ON THE ROAD TO ECONOMIC FREEDOM

An Agenda for Black Progress

ON
THE ROAD
TO ECONOMIC FREEDOM

An Agenda for Black Progress

edited by

Robert L. Woodson

REGNERY GATEWAY
Washington, DC

LIBRARY OF CONGRESS CATALOGING-IN-PUBLICATION DATA

On the road to economic freedom.
Bibliography: p.
1. Afro-Americans—Economic conditions.
2. Afro-Americans—Social conditions   I. Woodson,
Robert L.
E185.8.05   1987   305.8'96073   87-9823
ISBN 0-89526-578-8

Published in the United States by
Regnery Gateway
1130 17th Street, NW
Washington, DC 20036

Distributed to the trade by
Kampmann & Company, Inc.
9 E 40th Street
New York, NY 10016

Designed by Irving Perkins Associates

10 9 8 7 6 5 4 3 2 1

ACKNOWLEDGMENTS

Maintaining enthusiasm and support for new ideas is often a difficult task. Therefore, it is with gratitude that I thank all of those who offered challenges, guidance, and support for the new ideas and approaches expressed here.

The Anschutz Foundation, in particular, must be singled out for its role as catalyst in originating the idea and framework of this book, as well as for providing the financial support necessary to make this book a reality. Special thanks also to production editor Pamela Taylor; advisers, Heather M. David and Maria Downs; and for her skilled preparation of many drafts of the manuscript, Evelyn Hall.

Above all, I wish to thank the scores of local leaders and residents in neighborhoods across the country who have already put many of these new ideas into place by initiating community-based, self-help programs that represent viable alternatives to welfare dependency and despair.

Robert L. Woodson

CONTENTS

PREFACE

A new generation of black Americans has come of age since the civil rights movement reached its zenith more than two decades ago. It is a generation that has been shortchanged.

The tragic statistics that describe black America today serve as an ironic ending to an era of racial progress thought to have been ushered in by passage of the landmark Civil Rights Act of 1964. Black youth unemployment is up 20 percent; more than half of all convicted felons are black; and educational attainment among black Americans is despairingly low.

Although black Americans comprise nearly 11 percent of the country's population, the number of black elected officials, despite a dramatic rise over the last 20 years, represents only about one percent of the nation's total. And in stark contrast to a black consumer buying power equivalent to the gross national product of Canada (about $130 billion), only a tiny fraction of this nation's nearly 15 million businesses is black. In fact, the black business formation rate, palsied by lack of capital, is well below that of other ethnic groups making their homes within U.S. shores.

In short, black Americans are more socially, politically, and economically disenfranchised than they have been for more than a century. This grim reality lies in the wake of one of the hardest fought legislative campaigns against racial discrimination in the history of the free world.

Can racism be held wholly responsible for black America's social and economic distress? Can the pace of black progress be determined solely by the largess of white America?

Although racism still taints the American character, the contention of most civil rights leaders that its eradication is *the* precondition to black advancement is, at best, a confession of impotence and, at worst, a retreat from responsibility.

Historically, substantive gains have been achieved in spite of racial barriers—and by a black community that *had* to rely on its own resources to survive and prosper.

The record is also clear on the notion that government money is the key to solving all black problems. Since 1964, the federal government has poured billions of dollars into employment, housing, public welfare, and economic development programs designed to help the poor. The main beneficiary of this massive effort, however, has been the "social service industry," which has administered aid programs at salaries and fees that consumed the lion's share of allocated monies.

These programs have not worked. The poor, in even greater numbers, are still with us. A permanent underclass of more than one-third of all black Americans, unskilled and undereducated, remains untouched by civil rights gains, the war on poverty, increased black political power, and a mammoth social welfare industry.

An alarmingly high number of blacks have also developed a welfare dependency on government programs that, while providing a bare minimum cash source, both subsidizes poverty and saps individual initiative.

Over the last twenty years, there has been an absence of serious debate regarding the future direction of black America, especially its growing underclass. It is our hope that this book will inspire the kind of soul-searching generated by the likes of W.E.B. Du Bois, Booker T. Washington, Henry Highland Garnet, Frederick Douglass, Martin Luther King, Jr., and others concerned with formulating a black American agenda that contributes to the health and spirit of the entire nation.

In the 1983 publication, *A Policy Framework for Racial Justice*, a number of black scholars and members of the Black Leadership Roundtable argued that "the most urgent problems facing the excluded black can be addressed by focusing on three areas: the progress of the economy, the condition of the black family, and educational opportunity. They provide a framework for constructing solutions to the real, structural failures in the society and not just the superficial cracks and tears." They went on to say: "Americans must face the likelihood that greater—not less—government intervention and planning are required to revitalize the national economy."

While the writers of this book agree that the economy, family, and quality education are essential to reversing the current isolation and deprivation of black Americans, they repudiate the widely held notion that government solutions are intrinsically better and more effective than self-help entrepreneurial strategies that tap resources within the black community.

It is beyond the scope of this publication to attempt an analysis of all the interwoven elements leading up to the current crisis in black America. Rather, the authors have constructed a developmental agenda that examines ownership and new business development, educational alternatives, and the strengths of the black family as key ingredients to reversing the plight of the black underclass.

The National Center for Neighborhood Enterprise (NCNE)

was founded on the belief that policies based on local approaches, where the beneficiaries play a key role in the social and economic restitution of their own communities, should replace ineffective maintenance programs that produce dependency. Organizations that owe their origin to local initiative and spirit are much more likely to succeed.

This book is an outgrowth of NCNE-convened meetings over the past three years involving black Americans who are dedicated to exactly such a policy agenda—that is, one that builds on our own resources.

Development for any people begins with the belief that development is possible.

Robert L. Woodson

FOREWORD

The way we talk about racial justice evokes a sort of central bank, managed by the government, whose charge is to ladle out equal portions of everything to everybody.

We speak of income gaps, education gaps, test-score gaps, even life-span gaps, not merely to describe but to accuse. The gaps are proof of racism, and the government ought to do something to close them (though we are seldom clear as to just what the government ought to do).

The problem with this approach is that it puts the remedies to black America's problems outside black America. It encourages the belief that to attack racism as the cause of our problems is the same thing as attacking our problems. And so we expend precious resources—time, energy, imagination, political capital—searching (always successfully) for evidence of racism, while our problems grow worse.

This is particularly true for the black underclass, growing numbers of whom are caught in a seamless web of joblessness, inadequate education, family deterioration and spiritual decay.

Is there a way out? Maybe. *On the Road to Economic Freedom* offers at least a possible route from where we are now to where we should be.

Without sleight-of-hand, spinning mirrors, or raids on the national treasury, the authors suggest ways in which black America itself can take the lead in curing what ails us. Selected by Robert Woodson for their expertise, knowledge, and practical imagination, these men talk about what will work—or is working—to bring the poor and economically disfranchised into the American mainstream. They offer new ways of approaching some of our most intractable problems.

Paul Pryde, Robert Hill, Glenn Loury, and Robert Woodson spend little time on racism, choosing to devote their efforts to things they can change. Their priorities are economic development, education, and the black family. Theirs is no zero-sum redistribution game in which blacks can gain only at the expense of whites, but a wealth-creation agenda. *On the Road* offers some good ideas, but perhaps more important, it provides a fresh approach to some very tough problems.

William Raspberry

O N E

A Legacy of Entrepreneurship

BY ROBERT L. WOODSON

The story of black America as a winner, not a whiner, has been lost. Its historical zest for free enterprise, self-assertion, and open debate within its ranks is a peculiarly American story of trial, tribulation, and triumph.

In the past, the black community had to rely on its own resources to survive. Black advancement was inextricably linked with black self-determination. With a sassy and fearless newspaper published during the height of slavery, with entrepreneurs ready and willing to purchase a slave's freedom or guarantee his safety after escape, with the formation of all-black towns and the building of a self-sustaining support apparatus, black Americans exhibited backbone, resolve, energy, vitality, creativity, innovation, and intellect at a time when the country, was generally either indifferent or hostile to black interests.

Black communities, because of Jim Crow laws and practices, evolved into viable societies with their own hospitals, banks, restaurants, insurance companies, food and clothing stores, gas stations, moving companies, and other essential enterprises needed to maintain a community's viability. Black newspapers reported on the community's life, black doctors tended the community's sick, and black undertakers buried the community's dead. Black film theaters, inns, and hotels thrived at time when racial segregation was a fact of life and law.

Before the American Revolution, before slavery, and indeed, before the Mayflower, blacks had entrenched themselves as workers and entrepreneurs determined to make good in this new land of opportunity.

During the 17th and 18th centuries, free blacks owned inns, stables, construction firms, barber shops, tailoring and catering establishments, restaurants and taverns. They had ventured into shipbuilding, furniture and machinery manufacturing, real estate, and newspaper publishing. The total personal wealth of free blacks on the eve of the Civil War has been conservatively estimated at $50 million—$25 million in the South and $25 million in the North and West.[1]

At an 1889 Conference on Black Business held at Atlanta University, educator John Pope declared, "It seems to me that the mightiest privilege, the greatest blessing and the highest point of development which any man can seek is being an interested and controlling member in the foremost matters of his own country."

Hope's remarks were made during the time of a black entrepreneurial explosion that saw the formation of banks, insurance companies, savings and loan associations, and wholesale food supply houses. A black businesswoman, Madame C. J. Walker, would soon become one of the first of her sex to become a millionaire.

This juggernaut of self-generating black progress continued throughout the early years of the 20th century with a chain of retail stores and church-financed multi-million dollar book publishing houses. Hell-bent on seizing opportunity wherever it existed, the bustling of black business activity continued unabated until the Great Depression. And even then, although many black businesses failed, community support networks coalesced and became stronger. The World War II years and the extended postwar economic boom would set the stage for a new offensive by the black community to weave itself into America's socioeconomic fabric.

Black America would eventually become derailed, however, but not before the evidence was in that slavery, Jim Crow laws, lynchings and race-baiting politicians could not kill the community's collective will and determination to leap over barriers to accomplish its goals. Seemingly, the more restrictive the political, social, and economic barriers, the more determined black America became in its resolve to overcome them. And progress, for the most part, came about because it took its matters into its own hands.

The Early Decades

The social forces that have shaped the progress achieved by black America have been determined, in large measure, by the quality of debate within its own ranks.

In 1832, free blacks from around the country held a national black convention in Philadelphia to discuss new, state-legislated disenfranchisement laws, strategies for advancing the race, and ways of bringing about an immediate end of slavery. It was here that the first great debate occurred around the then controversial question of colonization—whether to stay in America and fight for self-determination or whether to resettle in a "colony" outside of this country to pursue black interests. In the end, the delegates voted with applause and shouts. "Stay," they chanted. "We shall stay."

The next great debate raged when famed abolitionist Frederick Douglass and the most radical black abolitionist Henry Highland Garnet met at an 1843 national black convention.

3

Garnet argued forcefully for slave resistance and self-determination to break the system of disenfranchisement. Douglass countered by counseling patience and "moral force." The lionized Douglass barely swayed the delegates from endorsing Garnet's speech.

Siding with Douglass out of deference was one thing; following him on this issue, however, was quite another. When the Fugitive Slave Law of 1850 was passed, the number of free black vigilance committees that were set up to aid runaway slaves actually increased. Despite the risks, these committees supplied fugitive slaves with lodging, clothing, medicine, and letters of introduction for employment.

Against the Odds

Free blacks (and some former slaves) more than held their own in the face of seemingly insurmountable odds. Many black businesses were fire-bombed, and their owners were tarred and feathered.

Even more seriously, free blacks were systematically stripped of their rights. They were disenfranchised in Delaware, Kentucky, Maryland, Ohio, and New Jersey. Between 1814 and 1861, they were either denied the vote or drastically restricted in their access to it in Connecticut, New York, Rhode Island, Pennsylvania, Indiana, Illinois, Michigan, Minnesota, Wisconsin, Iowa, Kansas, North Carolina, and Tennessee.[2] Black necks were on the line. Despite this, the zeal for freedom and the entrepreneurial spirit burned brightly in a community that refused to concede defeat.

During this year of punitive "Black Codes," the first black bank was incorporated in Washington, D.C. Two years later in 1890, Alabama Penny Savings Bank of Birmingham was opened, boasting 10,000 investors. The bank's officers confidently opened branches in Montgomery, Selma, and Anniston.

Other black banks and savings & loan associations would soon open in Illinois, Ohio, and Pennsylvania.

A surge of black business activity resulted and at the turn-of-the-century produced two companies that would eventually make *Black Enterprise* magazine's largest black businesses list—C. H. James and Company, a wholesale food supplier, and North Carolina Mutual Life of Durham, an insurance company. North Carolina Mutual today employs over 1,000 individuals and has current assets exceeding $200 million.

These new entrepreneurial conquests in banking, insurance, and real estate would have positive long-range effects on the concept of black self-reliance. Black businesses hired black employees. Black banks granted loans to prospective black businesspersons, landowners, and homeowners. Blacks were now able to purchase insurance, buy homes, and rent apartments.

In 1900, Booker T. Washington founded the National Negro Business League (still in existence) to promote and encourage black-owned business; some 400 blacks from over 30 states attended the group's first meeting in Boston.

Members of Washington's business league formed the Afro-American Realty Company in 1905 and, practically singlehandedly, turned white Harlem into a black metropolis. Masterminded by New York realtor Phillip Payton, the company, with a capitalization of $500,000 at $10 per share, bought up apartment houses and rented to blacks. And within a very short time, blacks soon owned and controlled more than $60 million in Harlem real estate.

The early 1900s also produced the phenomenon of scores of all-black towns such as Mound Bayou, Mississippi; Nicodemus, Kansas; and Boley, Oklahoma. The founder of Langston, Oklahoma, stated bluntly that these towns were created for the purpose of allowing blacks to "rule supreme in [their] own community."[3] Boley, Oklahoma, still in existence, had a population of 4,000 at the turn-of-the-century. Governed and run by

5

blacks, the town, at that time, had a bank, twenty-five grocery stores, five hotels, seven restaurants, a water works, an electric plant, four cotton gins, three drug stores, a bottling works, a laundry, two newspapers, two colleges, a high school, a grade school, four department stores, a jewelry store, two hardware stores, two ice cream parlors, a telephone exchange, five churches, two insurance agencies, two livery stables, an undertaker, a lumber yard, two photography studios, and an ice plant.[4]

The Harlem and Boley experiences, which matched aggressive black entrepreneurial activity with the self-assertive drive of the black masses, was multiplied nationwide to the point that in 1913, fifty years after emancipation, black America had accumulated a personal wealth of $700 million. As special Emancipation Day festivals and parades were held that year in cities and towns across the country, blacks could take pride in owning 550,000 homes, 40,000 businesses, 40,000 churches, and 937,000 farms. The literacy rate among blacks climbed to a phenomenal 70 percent–up from 5 percent in 1863. Booker T. Washington observed that black hunger for education was "unquenchable." And in this anniversary year, that was particularly evident, with 35,000 employed black teachers and 1.7 million black students enrolled in public schools.[5]

The Great Migration

The year of Booker T. Washington's death, 1915, also saw the death of his earlier "cast down your buckets where you are" philosophy. Self-determination beat so strongly in the breasts of the southern black masses that they began the Great Migration to the North in search of jobs and financial opportunities. Nearly 1.5 million blacks moved out of the South over the next fifteen years.

New industries created by the First World War, an end to

6

European immigration, and, above all, the trumpeting of the northern black press to "come on up" spurred this great movement of people determined to seize opportunity. Harlem, Chicago, Philadelphia, Pittsburgh, Detroit, and other cities absorbed the human waves and this new constituency and, in turn, created more black businesses.

The work was in the North. In its factories, stockyards, and service enterprises, blacks became garment workers, butchers, tailors, and barbers; many immigrants brought their own capital with them and established their own businesses. Chicago had five hundred businesses on the eve of the Great Migration; by the end of it, nearly four times that number were in operation. In fact, by 1920, Chicago became an active home-base for one-third of the country's black manufacturers. The city's black-owned factories turned out toilet goods, cosmetics, clothing, caskets, and mattresses.

To escape the crush caused by the extreme housing shortage in the cities, many migrants, like the frontiersmen before them, felled trees, cleared wooded areas, and created their own communities in Pennsylvania, New York, New Jersey, Ohio, Illinois, and other states. These suburbs and exurbs gave life to their own entrepreneurial class of garage owners, merchants, employment agency operators, and others who grew and thrived in new communities.

Amid this human flux arrived black capitalist Marcus Garvey who immediately sized up the situation. On his first visit here, a few months after Booker T. Washington's death, Jamaican-born Garvey noted: ". . . the people of the race (black Americans) have sufficient pride to do things for themselves."

Garvey, after traveling through many of the cities, was impressed by the number of colleges, banks, stores, cafes, restaurants, hotels, theaters, and real estate agencies that were owned and supported by blacks. This was, he decided, the country where he (and his organization) should be headquartered.

7

Tapping the longing of black people for self-determination, Garvey created an empire within a few years. By 1919, his Universal Negro Improvement Association operated grocery stores, restaurants, tailor and dry cleaning shops, and a publishing house. The jewel in the crown, however, was the Black Star Steamship Line, capitalized at $10 million by selling $5.00 shares to black investors. Unfortunately, all the ships purchased for the line were money-gobbling dinosaurs that eventually bankrupted the company. But Garvey understood that blacks wanted to invest in self-reliant, black enterprises.

Garvey was but one manifestation of the coagulating political, social, and economic needs of the new, black urban enclaves. As new roots were put down, black churches took over synagogues and the churches of white congregations, black doctors opened hospitals and clinics, black dentists and lawyers put out their shingles, black entrepreneurs bought out white businesses, and black politicians mustered black votes to become members of previously all-white inner city councils and state legislatures.

The new black presence fought back at lynchings and mob violence with a network of newspapers and magazines, enraged politicians, militant unions, combative lawyers, and an ever-growing sense of collective self-worth that could not be snuffed out.

This self-worth deepened and blossomed as the years wore on. In 1926, the total assets of black banks totaled $13 million, black art and literature reached a new peak by gaining a worldwide audience, and Mordecai Johnson became the first black president of Howard University, where he would soon hire black scholars and thinkers such as Ralph Bunche in political science, E. Franklin Frazier in sociology, Charles R. Drew in medicine, John Hope Franklin and Rayford Logan in history, and Charles Houston in law—all of whom would conquer their respective fields and leave legacies to unborn generations, both black and white. The *Chicago Defender*, a pillar

8

of the black press, was now being housed in a new $250,000 plant.

The Depression Strikes

With nearly 65,000 blacks owning businesses nationwide on the eve of the Depression, black America had dug in its heels and declared itself part and parcel of this country. It did not consider itself a separate nation of invisible men and women.

It had pulled itself together by taking advantage of every opportunity and listening to its own counsel. Black America had discovered the value of organization and collective strength.

As the country stood poised on the brink of economic catastrophe, black America, up to that moment, could claim that every segment of its community had chipped in to contribute to its survival. As it plotted slave rebellions and mapped escape routes during slavery, black America continued to formulate agendas and develop courses of action after its community had attained freedom. Scholars, businesspersons, laborers, ministers, servants, and professionals—all had their eyes on freedom and making it work for black people.

By early 1929, months away from the country's economic collapse, black America had made great strides: the Great Migration had put in place thousands of blacks in industrial positions in northern cities; the NAACP and its cadre of lawyers had won important court victories on the issue of black civil rights; Alexander Crummel's American Negro Academy was busy promoting black literature, science, and art, and, in scholarly articles and monographs, defending blacks against printed racist attacks; Carter G. Woodson's Association for the Study of Negro Life and History was in its fourteenth year of collecting sociological and historical documents dealing with the black American experience; agricultural chemist

9

George Washington Carver, while at Booker Washington's Tuskegee Institute, was finding industrial uses for the sweet potato, cotton, pecan, and the peanut that would revolutionize the agrarian South; A. Philip Randolph's Brotherhood of Sleeping Car Porters was still battling the Pullman Company and the American Federation of Labor for union recognition (Randolph would win his fight); and black churches had begun to purchase apartment buildings to open up housing for blacks in congested areas.

Black America even had its own unofficial national anthem. Written by diplomat/poet/author/civil rights leader James Weldon Johnson and scored by his brother J. Rosamond, *Lift Every Voice* began:

> *Lift every voice and sing*
> *Till earth and heaven ring*
> *Ring with the harmonies of Liberty. . . .*

The end of the decade, of the jazz age, saw black America making its presence felt, invited or not, into the nooks and crannies of American life.

And then the economic roof fell in on the country.

The Great Depression laid the nation low. One out of every four black workers was unemployed. Blacks were fired from their traditional jobs as bellhops, porters, janitors, waiters, elevator operators, and kitchen helpers while whites were hired in their places. *Amos 'n' Andy*, then the most popular radio show in America, depicted the misadventures of scheming, grammar-butchering Harlem blacks. Even its lead characters were played by white men.

W.E.B. Du Bois, one of the original founders of the NAACP, continued the tradition of black debate while editor of the organization's magazine, *The Crisis*. He had become so disenchanted with the devastating effects of the Depression on black America that he came out publicly for a separatist society in which black America devoted all of its energies to creating all-black businesses, communities, and farms to build "a strong foundation for self-support and social uplift." The apoplectic NAACP executive officers argued that "voluntary isolation would (bring about) a permanent secondary status." Du Bois and the NAACP officially parted company.

The extended family concept, a mainstay of slavery, was revived nationwide as unemployed aunts, uncles, and cousins moved into the households of traditional family units. Clothing, mended and altered, was passed down and around by people who had to share to live. Families lived on credit extended by the neighborhood grocer. Usually half the bill was paid at the end of every month; the other half would be carried over for as long as it took the consumer to catch up. Quite often, a number of years passed before this feat could be accomplished.

In the South, many blacks grew their own food, and swapped and shared with neighbors. The independent black farmers fared better than the penurious sharecroppers who fled the South in droves. And, as usual, the black churches and fraternal organizations served as gathering points for food, clothing distribution, and job information.

Scores of black moving and storage firms entered the ranks of black entrepreneurial enterprises during this period of constant movement and displacement. Many of these firms are still in existence today.

The black press joined forces with the black church and community organizations in Washington, New York, and Chicago to mobilize pickets for "Buy Black" and "Spend Your Money Where You Can Work" campaigns. They shared the cost of posting bail for jailed picketers. The tactic worked, as white-owned establishments capitulated and began hiring blacks.

Father Divine and Daddy Grace,[6] rival religious leaders, competed in their efforts to absorb the black poor into their respective flocks. Both Grace and Divine operated many businesses that provided hundreds of jobs for the unemployed. Divine, who grew his own food at black farm co-ops, provided nutritious free meals for all who entered his churches.

White America, like black America, was also on the ropes. Franklin Roosevelt's New Deal battled the Depression by creating work relief projects that were designed to put money in the pockets of the country's poor and disadvantaged. Not since Reconstruction had the U.S. government committed itself so massively to tackling social ills and getting its citizens back on their feet. Dogged every step of the way by a Supreme Court that looked askance at the New Deal Programs, Roosevelt nevertheless hewed to his course and introduced project after project that would, he felt, get the country moving again.

The enduring legacy of Roosevelt's emergency relief efforts was the creation of a professional class of social policy bureaucrats and a corps of sociologists, psychologists, and social workers who, in effect, formed a social service industry with its own social status, goals, and interests—a situation that often worked against the interests of the poor.

The New Deal programs were shot through with racism. Although it is true large numbers of the black underclass benefited from employment or emergency relief projects, it is also true that they were paid less, hired last, and fired first.

Building from Within

A recent university study[7] has shown that most low-income residents, when faced with a crisis, turn to someone or some group in their neighborhood for advice and help. This was precisely the situation that existed in communities of black America during the Depression. Mediating structures, such as churches, neighborhood associations, and families stood between the private lives of individuals and the megastructures of large-scale programs. It is this phenomenon that gave the black communities across the land a cohesiveness of spirit and purpose during yet another time of setback and retrenchment. Rent parties, rummage sales, quilting bees, church socials, homecomings, lodge meetings, and neighborhood gatherings around a communal pot-bellied stove served to unify a community thrumming with the will and desire to survive.

Drugs had not yet penetrated black enclaves to sap the will and deaden the mind. A Joe Louis victory, like a Jack Johnson triumph of years before, could lift black America to heights of euphoria no dangerous drug could ever achieve.

Black politicians and appointed officials, activist ministers, officials of fraternal organizations, lawyers, representatives of the black press, the local business community, the Pullman porter, janitor, the postal clerk, and the unemployed huddled and planned ways to keep themselves and their communities afloat.

Black America had a War Department (Du Bois, the black press, the battling and victorious NAACP lawyers who included Charles Houston and Thurgood Marshall); Department of State (A. Phillip Randolph and the Urban League); and a Department of Health, Education, and Welfare (the churches and fraternal organizations.)

The March Deferred

This machinery was in place to greet the forties. One faction would deal with Roosevelt over employment practices; another would deal with the courts over restrictive covenants and the pursuit of quality education. Others would petition the military for permission to fight in another world war while yet another group would take to the streets to demonstrate against police brutality and local hiring policies. And then, figuratively speaking, they would all meet at the lodge and compare notes.

The black press, as outspoken as ever, ran a "Double V" slogan on its front pages throughout World War II—for victory abroad *and* at home. In 1940, black newspapers throughout the country joined A. Phillip Randolph and a large group of black clergymen, politicians, and civic leaders calling for a gigantic march on Washington to protest the lock-out of black workers from the country's war industries. President Roosevelt, anxious to stop a march that would show a disunited America to the world, persuaded his wife Eleanor and New York Mayor Fiorello La Guardia to talk with the march organizers.

Randolph and his supporters would not budge. Black America was ready to work for the war effort. If it was to be stopped from doing so because of discriminatory hiring practices, then it would protest in as dramatic a way as possible. Preparations continued for the march. Weeks away from the march date, Roosevelt signed a 1941 executive proclamation that forbade discriminatory hiring policies by businesses holding government contracts. Instead of marching, black America did what it wanted to do in the first place—it worked.

Gates were swung open to blacks at aircraft plants, shipyards, and steel mills. As they were absorbed into these jobs, black workers began joining the big industrial unions that had so relentlessly conspired to keep them out.

Independence Day, because of its patriotic significance, replaced Emancipation Day in the hearts of blacks as the day to celebrate freedom. Flags, parades, bond drives, rubber and cooking fat collections, as well as tots in sailor suits were as much a part of World War II black America as they were of white America.

Long work hours and the pressure of worry about loved ones overseas needed a healthy recreational release that was soon supplied by black entrepreneurs who opened resorts, dance halls, and nightclubs. Black bus charter services sprang up to supply the transportation needs of large groups and organizations.

Once again, while white America took scant notice, black businesses were making headway. By 1942, forty-four black insurance companies carried a half-billion dollars in insurance policies.[8] Community entrepreneurs would begin joining forces with lodges and churches to sponsor weekly outings for black children that included free films, food, and recreational activities.

Not even a black community under siege was ripped apart. The bloodiest domestic race riot of the war years occurred in Detroit in 1943 when white mobs, supported by the city's police department, engaged in violent battle against the black community for two days. Detroit's black community not only held its ground, but steadily increased in numbers over the years.

War's end did not kill the war boom, it simply gave way to the postwar boom that kept the American economy perking for another ten years. Jobs were plentiful, and blacks snapped them up whenever and wherever they could. The black quest for knowledge remained insatiable as black literacy and elementary school enrollments were approaching parity with the figures for Americans at large, while blacks in the country's colleges and universities nearly equaled the number of white students in Britain.[9]

The Black Press

The black community, after a second global war, was becoming even more self-confident and assured in its self-definition of who and what it was—mostly because of the entrepreneurs in the black press. Black America's role models began taking on the appearance of everyday people, a development that forged an even stronger sense of community. The black press made heroes of neighborhood folk—the mothers, fathers, uncles, aunts, cousins, and neighbors who fought off mobs; the workers who despite taunts, jeers, and abuse returned to the factory gates every day; the young men who marched off to war; the politicians and clergymen who organized boycotts and demonstrations to open up housing and employment; the educators who sat with students after school to make certain knowledge was digested; and the good people down the block who always looked out for (and reported on, if necessary) the neighborhood children.

The community's information pipeline was the black press. Since 1827, the black press had fought aggressively for equal rights with its crusades for community protest, solidarity, and betterment. Its independence assured because local black businesses provided the bulk of its advertising revenue, the black press operated without fear.

By the mid-1940s the black press was represented by scores of newspapers across the country: The New York *Amsterdam News,* the Cleveland *Call and Post,* the *Philadelphia Tribune,* the *Chicago Defender,* the *Pittsburgh Courier,* the Atlanta *Daily World,* and the Baltimore *Afro-American* are but a few of the black-owned newspapers that furnished employment opportunities, earned the respect of their readers, and turned a profit.

It was black America's hunger for more information about itself that would turn a young black Chicago entrepreneur into a folk-hero. John H. Johnson, reared in bleakest poverty, revolutionized the black communications industry in 1945 by giving black America its first national picture magazine featuring personalities and current events. *Ebony* hit home.

It was not the first black magazine. It wasn't even the first magazine put out by the then three-year-old Johnson Publishing Company. But it was only the second to enter the consumer field and the first to hit it big. The time was right for its glamour, the full-page ads of consumer goods, and the editorial emphasis on the positive aspects of black life.

Ebony, a financial bonanza for its owner, packed its pages with black role models in sports, entertainment, the law, education, medicine, architecture, politics, science, literature, and business. Its successful formula also launched the Johnson Publishing Company empire which, as of 1985, ranked as the number one black business in America.[10]

The splashy color covers of *Ebony* matched perfectly the mood of a black America rosy with anticipation of the future; *Ebony* willingly embraced the American dream and made it relevant to blacks.

Coins were jangling in pockets now. Savings had been religiously socked away. Jobs were plentiful. And there was the G.I. Bill.

Black Americans, in droves, took advantage of the G.I. Bill of Rights—a program that opened up unprecedented educational, housing, and employment opportunities to those determined to better themselves. Blacks overwhelmed colleges and universities at both the graduate and undergraduate level. In 1947, Washington's Howard University Medical School could accept only 70 new students from well over 1,000 qualified applicants.

Blacks on a large scale moved into electronics, medicine, the law, radio-tv repair, sociology and psychiatry, the arts and humanities, business administration and economics—virtually no field was untouched by black America's traditional "unquenchable" hunger for knowledge.

While zoot-suits were the rage and Nat King Cole crooned, thousands of young men and women, most beyond their teenage years, returned to school. Married couples with children found retirees in the neighborhood to babysit while they worked during the day and attended school at night. Postwar black America was busy with bustle and achievement. One job was often not enough for those who craved more out of life.

Sons followed fathers into steel mills; cousins living outside of a community where there was work were sent for by relatives. Bus and train tickets were mailed to bring first, second, and third cousins to the source of employment.

The 1940s represented a time when black America whistled its way home from work or school. Black Americans were now, with their bomber pilots and war heroes, solid citizens *en masse* in a conquering nation. The community's newsreels, magazines, and newspapers told it so. The battle ribbons brought home from war were prized by whole towns, indeed, a whole race.

The postwar economic boom set in motion thousands of new careers and hundreds of small black businesses. Racial antagonisms did not cease, poverty did not disappear, but when the forties came to a close, black people knew this country was good for them, and they were good for this country.

Rights and Wrongs

The 1950s saw an aroused black community intent on smashing the color line. The schools, department stores, lunch counters, theaters—all were fair game for picketing or legal action. Again, a concerted effort by many black groups working together caused racial barriers to drop. To lay the underpinnings in the long legal trek that culminated in the historic 1954 Supreme Court decision in *Brown* v. *Board of Education*, a courageous cadre of NAACP lawyers argued scores of cases in small towns and countries across the land. In each instance, they were protected, housed, fed, and supported by black communities.

Martin Luther King, Jr., using the church as his base, gained national attention in the mid-1950s with his Montgomery Bus Boycott success. During this period of racial ferment in the South, the black population in northern urban areas continued to grow as a recession began crippling the national economy.

The groundwork was being laid for the turmoil and turbulence of the 1960s as cities, unable to supply jobs and housing, continued to attract those seeking work. Overcrowded urban areas began to fester and seethe with the resentment of idle workers. Civil disturbances, boycotts, and protest marches set the tone for a civil rights push that took on a dizzying momentum that seemed unstoppable. The large and peaceful 1963 March on Washington for Jobs, Peace, and Freedom served as the movement's centerpiece for galvanizing the government into passing meaningful civil rights legislation.

The landmark passage of the Civil Rights Act of 1964 climaxed a movement that was steeped in the rich tradition of black resistance to racism and discrimination. This act would mark the end of an era for a civil rights agenda that preached the proposition that massive government assistance would bring about a massive change in the lives of the poor.

The Price

It is ironic that while civil rights gains were being made, the self-sufficient economic infrastructure of black America was being eroded. Small black firms, the backbone of the racially localized black economy, could not compete with the newly integrated, low-priced, large volume department stores, supermarkets, fast food chains, and shopping centers. Many black businesses became casualties of racial progress.

Government aid programs, it soon became clear, would also exact a price from the black community. These programs, from the beginning, did not address the problems of the poor with solutions that had the input of the poor. The poor and disadvantaged, if pulled into the government's social welfare industry machinery, were turned into passive "clients" to service and lead by the hand into poverty limbo. This government-knows-best policy herded low-income families into high-rise buildings that bred crime and frustration, discouraged the work ethic, fostered dependency on public assistance, and stifled the initiative of small entrepreneurs with programmed-to-fail bureaucratic restrictions.

Counterproductive and misdirected programs also exacted a price from government. According to the U.S. General Accounting Office, in 1984, $75 billion was spent on housing initiatives, $300 billion on welfare programs, and another $25 billion on economic development. Despite this massive commitment of funds to fight poverty, U.S. Census Bureau statistics revealed that blacks were three times as likely as whites to be poor. Just as damning are the results of studies that show that those who gained most from civil rights programs were middle-class blacks, not the poor blacks who were the movement's foot soldiers.

Self-Help Efforts That Work

Despite the price of disenfranchisement, lynchings, race riots, economic setbacks, misguided government programs, seething urban ghettoes, and the endurance of a thousand and one well-funded, but meaningless studies on the pathology of poverty, the true legacy of entrepreneurship still thrives in the black community.

Building on the past, the black church and fraternal organizations (see Chapter 3) have launched new ventures of such ambitious scope that they often require new alliances and partnerships, a renewed mustering of community resources. The black press has expanded into a broader-based communications network that now includes prestigious specialty magazines (particularly those dealing with business and commerce), diversified publishing houses, and top-rated and lucrative radio and television stations. Black businesses have moved into high technology industries and are conquering this field by the same hard-nosed determination practiced by their ancestors.

But it is the grassroots organizations that have blazed new trails across black America. As neighborhoods band together to control their own destines, previously unused talents and resources are now being tapped to foster a climate of economic and social advancement in what had been considered to be human wastelands.

Nationwide, nothing could so stikingly emphasize this point as the emergence of public housing resident management corporations. In Washington, Boston, New Orleans, St. Louis, Louisville, Jersey City, Minneapolis, Chicago, Denver, Tulsa, Los Angeles, Kansas City, Baltimore, Pittsburgh, Houston, and wherever public housing authorities have allowed residents to manage public housing units, dramatic changes have taken place—scores of small businesses and hundreds of jobs have been created, crime and vandalism have decreased, teenage pregnancy statistics have been reversed and fathers and husbands have returned to abandoned families. At the same time, administrative costs have been drastically reduced, vacant apartments repaired, and rent collections doubled and tripled.

Before the wave of resident management corporations (RMCs) swept the land, these same residents were looked upon as government wards who could not be trusted to think for themselves. Now operating multi-million dollar budgets, resident managers have turned crime-ridden hell-holes into healthy communities that place a premium on education, family, and self-motivation.

The Action Agenda

Blacks are at a turning point in history. The era of the great civil rights marches is over. Although passage of the civil rights legislation aroused hopes that blacks could finally enter the mainstream of society, this has proven to be more illusion than reality. Old strategies have run their course; new efforts must focus on ending dependence on government by encouraging the growing movement among blacks to, once again, rely on themselves for an improved life.

People who are now "protected" by government aid programs need instead to be empowered by them. Policies should be geared toward maximizing independence, economic opportunity, and freedom-of-choice for those receiving government-funded services. Regulatory and procedural barriers that prevent a community from starting its own schools, day-care centers, and adoption agencies, should be done away with.

This less restricted policy approach will make it possible for greater numbers of low-income black citizens to participate in the mainstream of the American economy. A policy that will encourage the development of black enterprises will strengthen the economic base of black neighborhoods and put more money into the pockets of the black underclass.

It is time to approach the needs of the black underclass from a different perspective—one that is cognizant of the existing strengths within the black community; one that recognizes the abilities and ingenuity of individuals and groups in handling their own affairs; and one that keeps government intervention to a minimum. Regardless of their educational backgrounds, those experiencing the problems of poverty must play a primary role in developing avenues of escape. Above all, the black community must disentangle itself from the welfare professionals whose primary objective has become the maintenance of clients. Those who purport to serve the black poor must be held accountable and must offer realistic programs that inspire self-help to alleviate the conditions of the underclass. The ultimate goal, after all, is economic independence and self-sufficiency.

Rather than accept solutions parachuted in by middle-class, professional service providers, black America must recognize and expand on indigenous, self-help neighborhood efforts. The originators of these self-help programs have unique, firsthand knowledge concerning the problems and resources to be found within their communities. They have established track records for effectively solving social problems by motivating their communities to develop innovative solutions to the problems of unemployment, substandard education, teenage pregnancy, gang violence, day-care, and other sources of community travail.

CASE STUDY #1:

The Legacy Revived: A Self-Help Design for Living

Kenilworth-Parkside, a 25-year-old low-rise, low-income public housing complex in Washington, D.C., now stands as a model of how motivated residents can transform a crime-ridden hellhole into a thriving, productive community.

Until a few years ago, the 464-unit development was plagued by drugs, crime, vandalism, and a soaring teenage pregnancy rate. As of 1982, 76 percent of its nearly 3,000 residents were welfare recipients. Kenilworth-Parkside had fallen into such a low state of disrepair and neglect that residents did not receive hot water or heat for one two-year period.

Life on the downslide was reversed in 1982 when the newly created Kenilworth-Parkside Resident Management Corporation assumed control of the complex's day-to-day operation under contract to the District of Columbia's Department of Housing and Community Development (DHCD).

The new corporation was responsible for collecting rents, maintaining the buildings and grounds, enforcing DHCD housing regulations, screening residents, maintaining accounting records, and developing policy. A management fee is paid to the corporation for the services performed under this contract.

The results generated by the new Kenilworth-Parkside management reflected the new community spirit being fanned and ignited throughout the complex. Within two years, the resident managers had reduced teenage pregnancies by 50 percent, reduced welfare dependency by 50 percent, reduced crime by 75 percent and *increased* rent receipts *130 percent.* Administrative costs were cut by 64 percent during the first year of operation by hiring residents, rather than outside "professionals," to perform all necessary property and maintenance services. Kenilworth-Parkside now generates enough revenue to absorb all of its operating expenses.

Using the entrepreneurial skills of the residents, businesses were established within the complex by the resident management organization to provide jobs for unemployed tenants. The businesses in operation at the complex include a co-op supermarket, a barber shop, two day-care centers, a health clinic, a snack bar and carryout shop, a thrift store, a catering service, a screen door repair shop, and a video arcade.

By exercising greater control and independence over many of the issues affecting them directly, the resident managers, under their director Kimi Gray, have not only taken residents off welfare by giving them jobs, they have also kept families together and sent youngsters off to college through strong social service programs.

In fact, Kimi Gray, can be credited with instilling community spirit into the complex as far back as 1974 when she began the "College Here We Come" program. Gray began checking into the availability of student grants and then, with the cooperation of the D.C. Superintendent of Schools, initiated community workshops and tutorial programs. Within seven months, 17 students were sent to colleges across the United States; today, with the program still going full blast, that number has reached 587. "College Here We Come" is currently staffed by two college graduates who went through the program. The program provides GED, remedial, and college-level tutoring in mathematics and English for residents of both the complex and the surrounding community.

Kenilworth-Parkside also provides family counseling, a free legal clinic, various support services for its senior citizens, job training programs, and a job referral service.

In 1983, as a result of its own initiative and efforts, Kenilworth-Parkside obtained $13.4 million in grants from the U.S. Department of Housing and Urban Development to renovate all apartments in the complex. With these funds, the resident management organization will contract with residents to install windows, replace doors, fix bathrooms and kitchens, and repair roofs. The money also will be used for the training of residents in various management areas.

Resident managers have succeeded in instances where the private sector and government initiatives have failed. The key to this success is their firsthand knowledge of the problems, needs, and preferences of residents. As the Kenilworth-Parkside example illustrates, resident managers, unlike conventional managers implementing regulations and policies, take a holistic approach to solving the problems of their low-income residents.

T W O

Investing in People:
A New Approach to Job Creation

BY PAUL PRYDE

In a land where trillions of dollars are generated annually by millions of businesses of every size, black unemployment statistics, stark and gloomy, stand out as an aberration.

Old-line government remedies and patchwork programs have not burrowed through to the black underclass of unemployables who breathe life into these figures, who, in fact, by their sizable numbers mock the ideals of this nation's free enterprise system. Yet, it is this very system that *could* supply the mechanism needed to involve the disadvantaged in the economic mainstream.

An investor's market approach that would link up minority inner city labor with adventurous young firms willing to tap a large job market could turn this bleak situation into a bright one. Investing in people for profit is an idea whose time has come. Financing the early stages of a business's development in an economically depressed area could reap rewards three-fold—for the investor, for the business, and for the community.

As ineffective government social service programs are

slashed because of current economic realities, a private sector initiative that reasserts the old values of self-determination, individual enterprise, and community pride could rescue thousands from nonproductive, jobless existences.

Incentives that encourage job-generating, young companies to grow and prosper in areas that are rich in human resources but lack economic activity could be the catalyst that halts the current business practice of avoiding the inner city.

The challenge to the risk-taking spirit of the entrepreneur and the speculative appetite of the investor goes beyond accruing potential monetary rewards, however. Both also have the opportunity to correct the process labeled by syndicated columnist Neil Pierce as the "economic resegregation" of America. According to Pierce, while thousands of potential office and industrial sites go begging in urban areas, companies have taken flight to the outer suburbs where new, high-priced housing has sprung up to accommodate a highly mobile white work force.

A Flat-Footed Black Economy

This inner city economic disconnection is a study in startling statistics. Recent U.S. Census Bureau statistics reveal that black families are three times as likely as whites to be poor. The number of female-headed families is on the increase, the unemployment rate for black females 18 to 19 years old, is well over 50 percent; and for black males in that same age group, just under. By 1985, the black male unemployment rate had more than doubled that of the white male population.

America's 14,731,000 business firms generated $4 trillion in 1977 (the last year for which these figures are available). The 231,203 black-owned firms accounted for less than 2 percent of this number. Most black-owned businesses operate with no full-time, paid employees, other than the owner, and fewer than 1 percent of these firms had gross receipts of more than $1 million.[11]

In 1968, when civil rights activities and programs were at their peak, no more than a dozen black-owned businesses in Harlem were capable of hiring ten or more people in an area where more than one million people resided.

Some 68 percent of all black firms deal in personal services and retail trade: food stores, dry cleaners, restaurants, service stations, funeral homes, and beauty parlors comprise the bulk of the businesses. Manufacturing, an industry geared to employing large numbers of people, is far down the list of black enterprises. The black church is moving into this area by initiating neighborhood economic development projects, but the challenge of mounting a full-scale effort to match up hard-core unemployables with risk-taking ventures that could prove to be profit-making bonanzas has not yet been attempted. Civil rights leaders, many plagued by myopia for the last 20 years, must share responsibility for the precious time lost to unoriginal thought and black economic stagnation.

Changing Times

Twenty years ago, when most of the current civil rights strategies were formulated, a series of events that would, once again, change the direction of the American economy were just beginning to have impact. Formidable foreign competition, new technology, and a national political climate that changed dramatically from liberal to conservative brought about socioeconomic transformations that wreaked economic havoc on the black community.

Ignoring these factors, civil rights leaders, generally, blamed racism as the sole cause of black economic calamity. But these facts show that many of the difficulties that blacks now face were not caused by racism alone. Equally responsible, if not more so, were the erratic economic shifts caused by impersonal market forces that cannot be controlled or anticipated.

When America dominated world markets for automobiles, oil, electronics, and steel during the 1960s, foreign competition hardly existed. But Big Steel's loss of markets over the last 20 years reflects today's dog-eat-dog reality of stiff foreign competition that has spurred America's decline in industrial might. Just two decades ago, young men and women could be confident of obtaining good-paying jobs with steel plants in places like Gary, Indiana, for example. Today, owing to increased competition from Japanese and European manufacturers and the decline in the steel content of automobiles, steel companies have let go thousands of workers, creating severe unemployment problems.

In 1964, the average steel worker's real income peaked after what had been a steady escalation; employers were enjoying steady sales and profits, and children were expected to be better off than their parents. Today, steel workers are unemployed or on indefinite furlough while their companies, locked in battle with foreign competitors, threaten the next generation of steel workers with a shrunken job market.

In Gary, Indiana, with its majority black population, the free enterprise system, thus far, has not created new, well-paying jobs at a rate fast enough to employ that city's growing labor force.

Twenty years ago, U.S. commercial bankers were still complacently pursuing the "three-six-three" rule—taking in deposits at 3 percent, lending at 6 percent, and teeing off on the golf course by three o'clock. Bank failures were so rare that in 1963, Wright Patman, Chairman of the House Banking and Currency Committee, observed: "I think we should have more bank failures. The record of the last several years is that we have gone too far in the direction of bank safety."

By contrast, as a result of deregulation and increased competition, 71 banks collapsed in 1984. To underscore the glut of fat, lazy banks, a recent study by Arthur Anderson and Company predicts that the number of U.S. banks will drop from 15,000 to under 10,000 by the end of this decade.

From 1961 to 1969 (except for a brief period in 1967), this country enjoyed steady economic growth. Walter Heller, Chairman of President Lyndon Johnson's Council of Economic Advisors, could speak confidently in 1964 of "fine-tuning the economy" through the judicial use of fiscal policy.

With or without Heller's knowledge, the economy was already being "fine-tuned" for blacks. The urban-to-suburban shift that reached its zenith during the sixties left many blacks in the cities stripped of industry and commerce. Federally financed highway programs and generous tax subsidies for homeownership and new industrial plants made investment in the suburbs more attractive than in the inner cities. Housing discrimination may have made it more difficult for blacks to move from old neighborhoods to new ones in the suburbs, but it did not cause the changes in job and plant locations.

This mushrooming of suburban economic development, still much in evidence today, need not spell economic disaster for the countless thousands of unemployed black workers left behind in what are now urban poverty pockets. Ideally, the existence of an economically depressed area such as Gary, Indiana, would challenge an entrepreneur who possessed grit and hustle.

Knowing that the loss of business and jobs in Gary would cause both property and labor to decline in price, a smart entrepreneur could create a new economic activity that would involve all of the area's resources.

Abandoned property could be bought, and a facility, built and staffed by formerly unemployed inner city labor, could become a goods production center for this new market.

As business improved, an entrepreneur's increased income

could be passed along to his workers in the form of higher wages, or, if not, his workers could be hired away by other firms moving into the area to compete for the entrepreneur's customers and his newly retrained labor force. In either event, unemployment would decline, wages would rise, and a once deteriorating area would be on the road to health. This scenario, of course, represents an ideal situation.

In the real world, current tax policy makes it more rewarding for entrepreneurs to peddle oil and gas tax shelters or convert apartment buildings into high-priced condominiums than to start new businesses. Also, government regulations often discourage workers on welfare from accepting or training for new employment. The rhetoric and strategies of the civil rights movement, with its emphasis on attacking racism, cannot alter this phenomenon. What is needed is a sound economic development agenda.

Economic Development and Growth

Economic development is the process of adjusting successfully to economic change. It is not the erection of new buildings in otherwise deteriorating urban neighborhoods, nor is it the same as economic growth. Economic growth is quantitative; economic development, by contrast, is qualitative. Economic growth has to do with how *much* is produced; economic development with *how* it is produced.

A community where rapid economic growth is taking place experiences expanded production and increased hiring. A community undergoing rapid economic development, however, is geared to creating new economic opportunities that take advantage of technology breakthroughs, fresh ideas, and expanded economic growth environments.

The dynamics of economic growth and economic development are often linked, however. Henry Ford's creation of the assembly line (a development event) precipitated the rapid increase of automobile production and worker income (economic growth) which, in turn, led to the need for a tire, auto repair, and parts industry (a development event).

In constructing an economic development agenda, one of the major tasks should be the laying of groundwork that will accelerate the process of adjusting to change. Unfortunately, the typical response of those affected by economic change is to attempt to stop it by turning back the economic clock—steel and auto executives demand legislative protection from Japanese competition; public officials advocate laws to prohibit companies from shutting down plants that are no longer profitable; auto workers seek legislation requiring that a percentage of all automobiles sold in the United States contain a set number of American-made products; and spokesmen for minority groups argue for the relaxation or recession of seniority rules that threaten recently hired black and Hispanic workers.

Demands for programs of protection (as opposed to ones of adaptation) are understandable but not likely to produce long-term economic security. What would have happened if, at the turn-of-the-century, a hypothetical American Association of Buggy Manufacturers, along with a Buggy Workers International Union, had succeeded in securing a punitive tax on the manufacturers of automobiles. In the short term, the jobs of hundreds, perhaps thousands, of stable keepers, blacksmiths, buggy whip makers, and buggy workers would have been saved. In the long term, however, the nation might have lost millions of jobs in steel and automobiles—two industries that have been the nation's engine of progress for most of the twentieth century.

The purpose of a development agenda is to allow buggy whip makers or blacksmiths to adapt successfully to changing times—to create new business opportunities and jobs to replace those that may be threatened by progress.

Job Creation

In his recent analysis of Dunn and Bradstreet data, David Birch of the Massachusetts Institute of Technology, found that the creation or disappearance of firms explained most changes in employment. He discovered that the rate of job loss is roughly equal throughout the country.

Faster growing dynamic areas actually lose jobs at a more rapid rate than declining areas. Houston, for example, loses more jobs more rapidly than Buffalo or New Haven but experiences faster economic growth because its business replacement ratio is higher, resulting in a lower job loss rate. In fact, a high rate of job loss characterizes all regions and metropolitan communities. On average, all areas lose 50 percent of their employment every five years. Thus, Birch concluded that the key to new economic activity and job creation is the rate at which businesses are formed and expanded to replace those that are lost—for whatever reason.

Birch also found that most new jobs are created by small, young firms and not by large, established corporations. Specifically, his study found that from 1969 through 1976, 80 percent of new employment came from the creation and expansion of businesses with fewer than 500 employees and that independent businesses accounted for half of all employment.

Studies by such organizations as the American Electronic Association (AEA) and the National Federation of Independent Businesses (NFIB) support the proposition that small, young businesses have generated significant employment. AEA discovered that employment growth rates were twenty to forty times greater among teenage firms (those 10 to 20 years of age) than among mature firms (over 20 years old).

There is also substantial evidence that small, young firms are a major source of technological innovation in the United States economy. Research by the National Science Foundation

34

(NSF) concluded that small businesses are responsible for half of "most significant new industrial products and processes." NSF also found that small, young companies produced 24 times more innovations per dollar spent on research and development than large companies.

These findings relate directly to the plan of action that should be followed to attack black underemployment. Under this plan, an increased rate of business formation within the black community would be a top priority. Japanese-Americans, for example, the group with the highest level of business ownership, are also the group with the lowest level of unemployment. Not surprisingly, the group with the lowest level of business ownership suffers the highest rate of unemployment —black Americans.

Business Formation and Expansion

If the formation and expansion of new firms and new economic activity is the key to job creation in a community, then it follows that a development agenda must be designed to correct whatever it is that may depress business start-up and expansion rates. The key, though not the only solution, is available capital and, particularly, risk capital. Risk capital is what an entrepreneur needs to meet payroll and operating expenses during the early life of the company. Risk capital, in short, can be used wisely or foolishly in the pursuit of dreams.

From evidence now available, it appears that approximately 90 percent of the risk capital needed by entrepreneurs to start businesses comes from personal savings, friends, family members, and business associates. (The Small Business Administration, by contrast, accounts for perhaps 1 percent of all new businesses financed.)

MIT's David Birch states, "The job-generating firms tend to be small and dynamic—the kind of firms banks feel very uncomfortable about." In short, the firms that can and do generate the most jobs are the most difficult to finance through conventional sources. The very spirit that gives them their vitality and job-creating powers is the same spirit that makes them unpromising partners for the development administrator.

The reasons for Birch's admonition are clear. Most current public programs (especially at the federal level) that provide financial assistance to businesses operate like a series of gigantic bank teller windows, each with clear limits on how much can be withdrawn, who can make withdrawals, and how the funds may be used. Ideally, queued up in front of each of these windows would be firms with good prospects for creating jobs, tax revenues, and wealth for their communities—but without adequate access to capital. Unfortunately, this is rarely what one finds. Rather, the firms at the head of the line are those most skilled at manipulating the withdrawal regulations (or, at minimum, on the best terms with the tellers).

Efforts to establish remedies for those who find themselves perpetually at the end of the line (blacks, in particular) often produce results that are not only unsatisfactory, but perverse. In order to prove that they are socially and economically disadvantaged enough to qualify for certain forms of government assistance, black and Hispanic entrepreneurs must often claim educational and employment deprivation so severe as to make any reasonable person conclude that they have absolutely no chance of succeeding in business.

Limited amounts of capital for rigidly defined purposes funneled through people whose jobs depend on the avoidance of controversy is not the appropriate system for financing thousands of new, risky enterprises that may eventually pay off in a big way. A system where a few public officials make blanket investment decisions is not needed. What *is* needed to finance these young firms is a system of private sector individuals, each possessing a different appetite for risk and reward, who will make entirely independent economic decisions. What is needed, in other words, is not an agency—but a market.

The forces needed to create this kind of "risk capital market" are entrepreneurs willing to locate in areas of high unemployment and profit-seeking investors undaunted by the prospect of financing potentially risky companies. In these United States, there is an abundance of both.

Raising Risk Capital

In order to create the supply of risk capital needed by firms in areas of high unemployment, upper income citizens should be encouraged to invest their capital in people. One inducement sure to find favor would be to allow individuals who invest in firms located in designated high unemployment areas to take an income tax deduction equal to the amount of the investment in the same year as the investment, much like we do our home mortgages.

To ensure that this incentive is used to encourage investment in small new firms—rather than in large ones—investors should be restricted to capitalizing firms with less than $2 million in total net worth. The taxpayer would be limited to an annual deduction of $100,000. Thus, an investor who puts $100,000 in a new health care company located in an appropriately designated community would be allowed a $100,000 deduction on his tax return for the year. Depending on the tax bracket, the investor would reap a benefit over and above the profit from the investment. An investor in the 50 percent tax bracket, for instance, would save $50,000 in taxes, a 50 percent investor's rate of return added to the profit accrued from the original investment.

If only half of the estimated 145,000 black households whose annual earnings exceed $80,000 were to take advantage of such a tax break by investing $5,000 in eligible companies,

37

over $100 million would flow into job-creating firms in inner city areas.

Business Development Districts

The availability of risk capital, a scarce resource, would undoubtedly motivate many entrepreneurs to open businesses in non-traditional locations. Money alone, however, will not persuade the head of a promising new computer company to build a plant where crime and vandalism are rampant, where employees are assaulted and inventory is stolen. By the same token, a community will not be friendly to a new business activity that encroaches on residents and other businesses. The answer to this twin dilemma is the creation of an environment that allows businesses to flourish without bringing about a negative disruption of community life.

In order to qualify for tax-favored financing, firms should be located in specially designated areas or business development districts similar to the enterprise zones proposed by the Reagan Administration and already adopted by several states. The districts should be located where there is an abundance of vacant and unused property (warehouse and industrial districts, for example, would meet this criteria). A ready work force is usually always available because these areas are often located near neighborhoods where large numbers of unemployed people live.

With an increase in the supply of risk capital and the availability of safe and relatively inexpensive sites for plant location, new businesses would be attracted to areas they now avoid.

As the market for space in old industrial areas begins to grow, developers could convert old structures into "incubator facilities" to be shared by several growing companies. Within a few years, 50 to 100 companies could be housed in centrally located structures within each business development district.

Many of the new firms, of course, would either fail or grow slowly. A few, however, would experience explosive growth creating hundreds of jobs. At the end of a three year period, it is conceivable that thousands of new jobs might exist where once there had been none. Some of these new jobs would, undoubtedly, go to technicians and managers who live outside the immediate area. For entry level workers, however, many companies could take advantage of the disadvantaged workers tax credit (discussed later) to hire employees from the surrounding neighborhoods.

Nearby residential and commercial areas would benefit. Jobs in housing renovation and construction would increase because some workers would want to live near their jobs. Retail and service businesses, some started by low-income people with income maintenance funds, could capitalize on the purchasing power of employees of the business development district. A rundown area would start to take on new stability. New shops, improved housing, and other amenities would revitalize the district to the extent that other companies would be attracted to the area.

The existence of business development districts in cities throughout the country would encourage the start-up of thousands of new businesses. Many firms that would have failed from undercapitalization would now succeed, and many companies that would have formerly located in suburban communities would now move to inner city areas.

The change would be small, perhaps as little as 1 percent of the 600,000 new firms formed in the United States each year. But in absolute terms, the shift would be enormous. Year in and year out, firms that might not have been started, might have failed, or might have located elsewhere, would now be organized development districts.

Money pouring into risk capital pools aimed at these firms could reach $200 million annually, a mere 2 percent of the total now invested in various tax avoidance schemes. Some new firms, many black, would grow rapidly. At the end of ten years, more than 60,000 firms and 3 million workers could be located in business development districts.

Hiring and Training Workers

Residents of neighborhoods adjacent to business development districts would be the immediate beneficiaries of such a surge in economic activity. To ensure this goal, incentives that would make it attractive for growing firms to hire and train inexperienced workers should be implemented.

One segment of this population that should be targeted is the large pool of untrained, young black workers—a powerhouse of untapped labor.

Despite the fact that most workers are trained on the job, many employers refuse to hire unskilled black youths because they are perceived to be too great an investment risk. This prevailing attitude is underscored by the staggeringly high percentage of willing-to-work black youths who have not been assimilated into the country's labor market.

Too many employers believe that black youngsters in inner city neighborhoods are poor investment risks and that their work habits, attitudes, and poor education make it unlikely that training investments will pay off. In many cases, this thinking represents pure racism. But, unless an employer's fears can be overcome, black youngsters will have great difficulty securing jobs that are created literally in their own backyards.

The Reagan Administration's most recent enterprise zone proposal contains incentives that should be useful in overcoming this problem. The bill gives employers a tax credit for hiring disadvantaged workers that starts at 50 percent and declines to zero at the end of seven years. Thus, an employer who pays an eligible worker $10,000 in the first years of employment would reduce his federal tax by $5,000 annually. For many new, small companies, this approach has obvious benefits.

This incentive could also prove beneficial to struggling young companies if the tax credit could be sold or carried forward and applied to a later tax liability.

Some companies could use tax credit in another way. Savings resulting from the tax credit could be used to buy the recruitment, screening, and support services of local community organizations that, demonstrably, can reduce hiring mistakes, supply disadvantaged workers with much-needed support, and alleviate the "hassles" normally associated with employment of undereducated and unskilled people. These strategies should both increase the number of growth-oriented firms in underdeveloped cities and swell the number of *young*, undereducated employees in the nation's work force.

The French and British Models

Even if all these incentives were implemented, substantial numbers of hard-core, inner city unemployables would remain untouched. Many will be black female heads-of-households with too many dependent children to obtain full-time training or work. Some will be older men, whose skills are limited or obsolete, making them dubious candidates for long term employment in growth-oriented companies. Both of these groups are probably receiving some form of public assistance. In dealing with them, a lesson may be learned from the British and French transfer systems.

France and England use maintenance funds, such as unemployment compensation, to attack unemployment directly by urging recipients to invest in job-creating businesses. Instead of subsidizing continued dependence, France allows any citizen who is entitled to unemployment compensation to collect six months of benefits in a lump sum to invest in a business. This program, begun in October 1980, was responsible for some 75,000 persons starting new companies. As of March 1983, between 60 to 80 percent of these businesses still survived.

A pilot "Enterprise Allowance" scheme launched in England in 1982 proved to be equally as successful in motivating individuals. Under this program, eligible unemployed persons may receive an allowance of $60 a week while working at least 36 hours per week to establish a business. In addition, participants must invest the equivalent of $1,500 of their own (it may be borrowed) in the new business.

These ideas are not new ones. In the United States, transfer payments have been used by thousands of people to start businesses. Welfare mothers, unemployed steel workers, and others receiving public monies have, on their own, launched successful small businesses.

Technically, however, these activities are illegal; although what they represent is good, old-fashioned American ingenuity, these undercover entrepreneurs risk punishment. These efforts at self-sufficiency should be rewarded and encouraged, not penalized. Recipients of unemployment compensation and aid to families with dependent children should be allowed to use these payments to start businesses, enroll in job training programs, or apply for the support services needed to obtain and hold full or part-time employment. Whatever is necessary to get them off dependence and make them self-sufficient should be the rule.

This useful and responsible approach would undercut the dependency syndrome that so often saps the will and deadens the motivation of those receiving public funds.

The Action Agenda

Burrowing through to the black underclass with a workable economic development agenda should be one of the country's top priorities. Despite past failures, the feat of turning a seemingly hopeless situation into a healthy one can be accomplished. A successful plan of action should include the following:

- People investing in the stock of small, young companies should be allowed an income tax deduction of up to $100,000 annually. To qualify, the company receiving the investment should be located in a designated business development district set aside for business expansion.
- Employers located in these areas should be given a tax credit for hiring disadvantaged workers. The tax credit should start at 50 percent of the employee's first year's wages and decline to 10 percent over a seven-year period. To increase its value to new companies, it should be permissible for the credit to be carried forward or sold to a third party. The credit could also be used to purchase worker training and support services from local community organizations.
- Recipients of public assistance payments should be allowed to use these monies to invest in a business or a job training program that would qualify them for full or part-time work. At the same time they should remain eligible for other in-place programs designed to put a person back to work.

The adoption of these proposals would trigger a series of actions that would complete the process of economic development. Accounting, law, and investment banking firms would begin to devise ways in which their high-income clients could invest in business development districts in order to take advantage of the new tax deduction. Investment partnerships would be formed to attract capital to finance companies that investment banking firms and venture capital firms found attractive. Companies such as Merrill Lynch and E. F. Hutton could send a prospectus to investors showing them how they might reduce taxes, profit from investment, and, at the same time, help decrease unemployment. Local officials encouraged by the promoters and managers of investment pools could designate old industrial warehouse districts near poor neighborhoods as business development districts. Mayors and city councils could act quickly because implementation would not involve significant local expense. And, the increased availability of substantial amounts of risk capital would encourage entrepreneurs to look for business locations within the designated development districts.

Marching will not lead black America to economic success. The road from poverty to empowerment is one of entrepreneurial risk and exploited opportunities.

THREE

The Black Church
and Community Empowerment

BY BILL ALEXANDER

The self-made men who founded the independent black church organizations in the 18th century were the first to introduce bootstrap economics to the black American experience. Pooling the scanty resources of runaway slaves and free blacks to purchase land and a building, these men heralded the beginnings of the oldest and most enduring black institution in America—the black church.

Its earliest concerns, rooted in the needs of an excluded and oppressed black population, focused on mutual aid societies that provided services and resources for the congregational community. Black entrepreneurship gained its legs through this church-led process of aggressive self-determination. Insurance companies, banks, publishing houses, newspapers, and a host of small businesses owe their existence to the economic muscle of the black church.

Today, that muscle is bulging. Black America's first organization now boasts a membership of 20 million and weekly collections of $10 million. Its 65,000 churches have a current estimated total value of over $10.2 billion.

45

An explosion of black church-inspired community development programs is now taking place nationwide. For the first time, denominations are putting aside religious rivalries and joining forces to attack poverty, unemployment, housing shortages, and ignorance. Black churches have escalated their commitment to the economically disenfranchised by targeting short-range programs to meet immediate needs and crafting long-range programs to empower and incorporate this group into energy-generating clusters of economic activity.

The vast majority of these new programs, some 90 percent, have been initiated solely with church resources. In addition to the traditional go-it-alone approach of the black church, many ministers automatically shy away from any fiscal arrangement with government agencies because of bad experiences. Bureaucratic red tape and loss of control are the two main reasons cited for avoiding collaborations with city, state, and federal agencies on community-building.

"We have sustained ourselves down through the years by pooling our nickels, dimes, and quarters at the corner church," comments Vinton R. Anderson, President of the African Methodist Episcopal Church Council of Bishops.

Anderson, one of the founders of Leaders Energizing Neighborhood Development (LEND), a pioneering new organization created to harness the talents and energies of the economically disadvantaged, believes that black Americans have "survived with dignity" because of the economic development policies instituted by the black church.

"With no government support in the early years and little government support in recent years, the black church has been the prime developer of opportunities and skills within our community," Anderson points out.

Current examples of black church economic power and the determination to invest in black America's future include:

- *The Congress of National Black Churches (CNBC)*, a coalition of the seven largest black denominations representing 14 million members, has joined in a precedent-setting alliance to bring about black economic parity. With the potential to generate accounts totaling $93 million a year, CNBC is establishing a nationwide collective banking and cash management program involving black banks and other minority firms. Six of the 34 planned church management service centers have been set up by CNBC to generate new businesses and jobs through collaborative ventures with local businesspersons.

  CNBC recently signed an historic agreement with the Aetna Life & Casualty Insurance Company creating a master insurance agency under the control of CNBC, the majority shareholder, which provides property, casualty, and liability coverage for more than 60,000 church properties. Known as the Church Insurance Partnership Agency, it is now developing group life and health insurance and retirement annuity coverage for 250,-000 CNBC church employees.

- *Leaders Energizing Neighborhood Development (LEND)* was founded in 1983 by senior officers of the African Methodist Episcopal Church. Allied with the National Baptist Convention, U.S.A., this organization has committed itself to minority economic development by starting up church credit unions in six cities. It has begun a security training program targeted for 13 cities that will create employment and combat crime in low-income areas. LEND has encouraged community entrepreneurship by offering three-to-one interest free matching funds and providing technical assistance and management training.

- *The United House of Prayer for All People* with 146 churches in 22 states has launched a major low-income housing program that will soon expand to 11 states. The House of Prayer (as it is commonly known) has invested $20 million of its own money for the construction of low and moderate-income housing in Charlotte, North Carolina; New Haven, Connecticut; and Washington, D.C. Minority contractors, building managers, support personnel, and those seeking affordable housing all benefit from this building program. The United House of Prayer finances many of the small businesses that are located in these new housing developments.

• Baltimore United in Leadership Development (BUILD) is an interdenominational group of 32 churches with a proven track record of bringing about inner city community empowerment. BUILD-affiliated churches have galvanized the city by conducting a campaign of coordinated research and negotiation that successfully rolled back automobile insurance rates for low-income residents by as much as $500. BUILD is now negotiating for special-rate renovation contracts for 1,000 vacant homes in order to make them habitable for low-income families.

• *The Southeast Cluster,* using the principle of "corner" economics, which builds up from the community rather than trickling down, was recently formed in Washington, D.C. It is located in the city's most economically underdeveloped area: Anacostia, where most of the low-income black population is concentrated. The 18 churches that comprise the cluster are now establishing a centralized credit union that will have a branch in each member church.

The Ambitious Corner Church

Homegrown church programs have traditionally coped with community needs. Family counseling, blood pressure clinics, day care centers, senior citizen activities, and family community events have always found a home at the corner church. But the community's heightened sense of economic awareness has pushed individual churches into new, bolder ventures that underscore the traditional leadership role of the black church in the area of economic development.

Telling examples of this "corner church" initiative can be spotted throughout the country:

- In Washington, D.C., the Reverend Willie F. Wilson's Union Temple Baptist Church has begun construction of a $2.5 million community center that will include a credit union, dinner theater, health spa, African Art Museum, bookstore, computer training school, and day care center. This new facility will be built in an economically depressed area.
- The pioneering multi-million dollar Family Life Center was built by Washington's Shiloh Baptist Church in 1982. With the dual purpose of correcting bad inner city health habits and strengthening the family, the Family Life Health Center has a sauna, four bowling alleys, racquetball courts, a roller skating rink, jacuzzis, family game rooms, and community conference rooms.
- In Jamaica, Queens, New York, the Allen Church (African Methodist Episcopal) purchased ten dilapidated stores for rehabilitation for $250,000 and, without any government aid, built a $3 million elementary school in an area where the crime rate is high and the school attendance low.
- In Oakland, California, the Allen Temple Baptist Church formed a federally insured credit union, built a 75 unit apartment building for senior citizens, purchased commercial property and, soon, will launch a human development corporation that will focus exclusively on economic development projects within the community.
- In Chicago, Illinois, with cash reserves of $1.1 million and real estate valued at $24 million, the Antioch Missionary Baptist Church has launched a $30 million community redevelopment program that will both build and renovate residential, commercial, and institutional facilities. Included in this massive investment package will be a senior citizen's apartment building and such commercial ventures as drug stores, grocery stores, restaurants, a barber shop, beauty shop, dry cleaners, and more.
- In Lafayette, Louisiana, the Reverend Roy L. Winbush of the Gethsemane Church of God in Christ has started a community credit union. "We have become aware of the spiritual and physical benefits derived from economic development," said Winbush.

- In Baltimore, Maryland, Bethel African Methodist Episcopal Church calls itself "The Church with a Heart in the Heart of the City." The church not only supports its own credit union but holds forums, seminars, and conducts a 13-week series of classes on budgeting, taxes, minority business, and mutual fund investment. The 5,000 member church, one of the oldest black churches in the country, is also involved in low-income housing and a food cooperative buying program that serves over 1,000 families each month.
- In New York's Harlem, the mighty Canaan Baptist Church of Christ, with federal assistance, built two 20-story apartment houses in a community in desperate need of housing for its low and moderate-income residents. Canaan also operates a credit union capitalized at $150,000 and a travel agency.

The New Phase

Today, more and more churches are going beyond traditional outreach and support programs to the higher ground of community empowerment. At the 1984 convention of the National Assembly of Black Churches, James E. Hurt, Jr., president of Black Church Publications, Inc., noted that "all we have to do is turn over our annual $200 billion earning power three or four times in our community to create 1.5 million jobs throughout black America."

An economic development package presented at the convention included programs to strengthen black banks and other minority businesses. It also included proposals to establish a National Church Bank, an endowment fund for black universities, and a national credit union.

Diversification has now become an economic priority for the black church. Using the management procedures of big business, blighted areas and human wastelands have been turned into sites for housing developments, shopping centers, factories, recreational and health facilities, bakeries, loan companies, publishing houses, day care centers, dry cleaning establishments, travel agencies, food cooperatives, printing shops, schools, health clinics, and job training centers.

The black church has, in effect, dropped its bucket right where it is—in the black community. Almost singlehandedly, it has fought off the corrosive encroachment of gentrification by either refusing to sell its property to realtors and private developers or by outbidding and buying up real estate for its own use.

Black Entrepreneurial Beginnings

The extent of the precedent-shattering move toward interdenominational cooperation and communication alone marks the 1980s as a landmark decade in the history of the black church. Bickering and feuding have been set aside to formulate aggressive economic policies designed to promote black fiscal solidarity. Future programs are breath-taking in their top-to-bottom *encompassment* of economic verities. Present-day programs are distinctive in their boldness and diversity. But it was during America's early years that the pattern was set for the black church's involvement in economic development activities.

During the late 1700s and throughout the 1800s, the black church was generally the only strategically placed major building owned by blacks in their community. These buildings became the focal point of black life. Formed out of protest to the segregationist policies of the institutionalized white church, the black church became a hotbed for the assertion of black humanity. Pent-up frustrations fueled the free black population into converting their created church structure into a countrywide network of political, social, and economic activism.

Energized by tough, gifted pastors who earned their living

51

as doctors, lawyers, educators, or tradesmen, the congregations made their church buildings and private homes the backbone of the Underground Railroad. Mutual aid societies were established to provide jobs, food, and shelter for runaway slaves.

The black church became the black family stabilizer. From the christening of the newborn to the burial society's financing of a funeral in the church cemetery, the black church was there to provide guidance and direction from the cradle to the grave. The Emancipation Proclamation was celebrated in the churches with the same all-out exuberance that the Fourth of July now commands. During this period, the black church reigned as the power force and source in black American life.

Despite powerful enemies, the black church had pulled its people through the most tormented period of the United States' young life. It created a black survival network where none had existed before. This first great phase of black church activity also included the founding of the two largest denominations as national entities—the African Methodist Episcopal and the National Baptist Convention conferences. The black church was now ready to get down to business. The two newly formed religious conferences began conducting their activist activities above ground by building and sustaining colleges and universities and sponsoring national black political conventions.

An important link was forged during this second phase of church activity with emerging black fraternal orders that began to lay claim to the loyalties and finances of the black population during the period 1865 to 1917. It speaks to the resiliency of the black church leadership that rivalries did not develop; rather, partnerships ensued that lay the foundation for the first black-owned banks and insurance companies.

Church mutual aid societies joined in ventures with the Masons of Mississippi, the Odd Fellows of Georgia, the Elks, and the True Reformers. These alliances produced the North Carolina Mutual Insurance Company and Atlanta Life. Between 1899 and 1905, 28 banks were organized by blacks. Some, like the Alabama Penny Savings Bank, had black ministers as their first presidents.

The Baptist and Methodist conferences, where the vast majority of the black population held membership, became big businesses unto themselves. Large staffs were employed to administer extensive real estate holdings and to tend the day-to-day affairs of a large organizational structure. Both conferences also built, staffed, and maintained missions in Africa from revenue contributed by member churches.

The Methodists and Baptists formed their own publishing houses to print and distribute church literature. Newsletters, church bulletins, circulars, and flyers, all went through a church-owned and staffed plant. The Baptists, by printing their own hymnals, launched the first $1 million publishing house. The *Afro-American* newspaper, which publishes today, began life as a Baptist newsletter.

World War I sparked a mass migration of black people from the rural South to the urban North in search of work. Families disintegrated as the quest for work led anywhere and everywhere. A brother stayed with relatives in Chicago; a sister boarded in New York. Southern churches suffered drastic drop-offs in memberships, while northern churches were overwhelmed with the task of attempting to cater to the needs of this sudden influx of people.

Religious or quasi-religious cults stepped into the breach. Marcus Garvey, a native of Jamaica, held his first public meeting in this country at the historic Bethel African Methodist Episcopal Church in Philadelphia.

And then came Father Divine. Like Garvey, he lulled a disoriented black population away from the established church. Divine's appeal was irresistible—free food, free lodging, and guaranteed employment. A brilliant young black man, whose given name was George Baker, Divine delivered his promise. From 1919 on, he began buying farms and buildings so that his organization could produce its own food and provide shelter for its followers. He created and staffed businesses such as dry cleaners, laundries, and restaurants. An empire was built.

Father Divine's Peace Mission Movement was equaled in influence among the black masses by only Bishop C.M. (Daddy) Grace's United House of Prayer. Grace, too, was a brilliant entrepreneur who capitalized small businesses and set up his own manufacturing and distribution network. Like Divine, he invested heavily in real estate. Grace's marketing techniques for products he manufactured bordered on genius. Not restricting himself to religious artifacts, as did Divine, Grace carved out a market in household and personal hygiene products. Daddy Grace toothpaste was a big seller in the black neighborhoods of the urban North during the thirties and forties.

The Black Muslims, at their peak, also provided a positive black entrepreneurial role for the community. Bakeries, dry cleaners, restaurants, a fishing fleet, and a well-equipped state-of-the-art publishing house that published what was then the largest selling black newspaper in the country—all came under the economic development umbrella of the Black Muslim movement.

Still absorbing the influx of black migration from the South during the Depression years, the black churches in the North were re-formed and positioned to become the bastions of power they are today. Their immediate task, however, was to stabilize their communities and neighborhoods so that effective black economic and social mechanisms could take hold.

One of the leaders in this effort was New York's Abyssinian Baptist Church and its charismatic pastor, Adam Clayton Powell, Jr. The church, located in Harlem was determined to smash rigid segregationist policies that kept out black businesses and prevented residents from securing employment in the most densely populated black community in the country.

Powell, solidly backed by church members and non-church members alike, took to the streets. He led daily protest marches, backed up by boycotts against area merchants. As had to be, agreements were hammered out, and a willful and determined church was granted economic breathing space. This tactic, out of life-or-death economic necessity, was repeated in other cities.

Powell, Martin Luther King, Jr., and many other black ministers brought the Underground Railroad above ground. Advising presidents, marching in the streets, and settling community economic disputes via mediation and reconciliation were necessary stops on the way to black economic freedom.

Social ferment, economic diversity, and racial agitation have always kept the black church's resources arrayed across many fronts. Politics, education, economics, and social and spiritual needs were constantly being juggled to accommodate the vicissitudes of black American life. The momentum of the Civil Rights movement of the 1960s, powerfully propelled by the black church, laid the groundwork for a sweeping new church-led approach to community empowerment on a national scale.

Moving On Up

The Opportunities Industrialization Centers (OIC) and the Zion Investment Corporation (ZIC) were the brain children of a group of Philadelphia ministers headed by the Reverend Leon Sullivan. In 1964, the Reverend Sullivan convinced the 5,000 members of his Zion Baptist Church of a need for a community-based employment and skills training program for black youth. The Zion congregation responded by raising $200,000 for a job training center that would provide services for youth from 400 other city congregations.

By design, Sullivan's concept has expanded to include the unskilled, unemployed, and disadvantaged of any age, sex, or race. OIC now operates job training centers in more than 200 communities in 42 states, Washington, D.C., and the Virgin Islands. Its current $100 million operating fund comes from the U.S. Departments of Labor, Commerce, and Education; major corporations; local and state governments; foundations and individuals.

With its staff of 5,000, OIC has trained over 640,000 persons, of whom approximately 79 percent are now employed. Its comprehensive employment training program now includes more than 160 different skilled areas: for example, banking, graphic arts, air-conditioning and refrigeration, bookkeeping, brick masonry, data processing, health care, computer operation, cosmetology, and auto body repair.

The Zion Investment Corporation, under Sullivan's stewardship, also became successful as a national, yet community-based, economic development project. Through a network of black churches and fraternal organizations, it offered individual shares for $360 each. To attract low-income investors, ZIC devised the 10/36 plan whereby shareholders paid $10 a month for 36 months.

Philadelphia-based ZIC invests $200 while $160 of the share cost is diverted to development in the investor's home community. Through its investment arm ZIC, OIC now owns shopping centers, housing developments, and an aerospace manufacturing plant.

It is significant that Sullivan and his congregation were off and running with OIC entirely on their own. Although many middle class Zion members were able to lay $300 and $500 checks in the collection plate, the enduring "nickels, dimes, and quarters" black church approach, once again, prevailed. It means, as it always has, snapping beans, preparing potato salad, and frying tons of chicken for the dinner fund-raisers; and, baking home-made sweet potato pies and seven-layer chocolate and coconut cakes for the bake sales. It means, as it always has, black people, from low-income backgrounds themselves, looking out for their own without fanfare or orchestrated publicity.

The Zion enterprise set off a prairie fire of public and private sector reaction. The black private sector, especially, responded wholeheartedly. The Prince Hall Masonic Temple of Maryland contributed $75,000 to the Zion Investment Corporation.

During the seventies, as OIC expanded and scores of church-inspired community development projects were taking hold around the country, the Baltimore-based Masonic Temple order joined forces with the Second Episcopal District of the African Methodist Episcopal Church and financed the construction of a $4.5 million low-to-moderate-income housing development in Baltimore's inner city.

Some Programs Sabotaged

Because of the iron hand of the Reverend Leon Sullivan and the solid base of support given him by his congregation, OIC hewed to its original intent and still stands as a model program of private and public sector collaborative effort. Other programs, however, that came on the heels of the civil rights protests of the sixties and relied on government assistance did not fare as well. In fact, many turned sour.

According to the Reverend E. V. Hill of Los Angeles, he and some 1,400 black ministers from around the country were approached by the Lyndon Johnson Administration about having their churches build low-income housing for the elderly and disabled. This tactic was designed to circumvent the difficulties encountered by city and state governments in passing referendums that would allow the building of low-income housing.

Hill was told that his Mt. Zion Church would receive 205 percent financing in addition to legal and other services provided by HUD to build the low-income Mt. Zion Towers in Los Angeles.

But, according to Hill, there were problems with HUD every step of the way. "Bureaucratic red tape snarled everything," he said.

The Mt. Zion project, located in Watts, did not qualify for government subsidized Section 8 monies; yet, the Black Stone Manor in Santa Monica, located in the affluent Wilshire district, did. The Mt. Zion Towers project land was worth about $40,000; however, the cost to the church was $175,000. In addition, the architects were paid double the fee originally agreed to, and the contractor ran over budget by $280,000.

Alarmed by this, the Reverend Hill refused to sign orders that would allow work to continue because, he insisted to HUD officials, his church no longer had the resources needed to complete the project.

Hill said HUD officials tricked him into signing by telling him that the church would not be liable for cost overruns. But, according to Hill, when the project was finally completed, HUD moved for foreclosure.

"At the beginning of the project, HUD promised to lead all the ministers new to this procedure by the hand, showing us all what we needed to know; at the end of my project, they wanted to foreclose," complained Hill.

Hill went to court to stop the foreclosure. Ruling in his favor, the court held that HUD had an obligation, based on its original promise, to work out an agreement with Hill's group.

Hill's experience was not an isolated one. At the end of the Carter Administration, more than 800 of the original 1,400 low-income projects initiated by the Johnson Administration had been sold (or had their assets transferred), foreclosed, or were in the process of foreclosure. Many of the projects were in foreclosure before they even opened.

"By doing this, HUD has hurt the good name and prestige of an entire segment of the black church leadership," said Hill.

The Eighties Explosion

From small community credit to multi-million dollar national economic networks, the black church has escalated its intent to marshal its resources to upgrade the quality of life in the black community.

Its power, collective intelligence, and money are being hurled against an economic situation so critical that to stay in place is to lose ground. The battle against the physical deterioration of neighborhoods, redlining, loan-sharking, usurious interest rates, and community cash outflow is an ongoing process that is in constant need of fresh, new, and bold approaches.

At the beginning of this chapter, several brief examples were given of new programs in place and working. A closer examination of some of these projects reveals the essential strategy of turning the dollar around several times in the black community so that residents will reap more benefits.

The Congress of National Black Churches (CNBC) by its very size commands attention. It is an affiliation of the seven major black denominations, representing approximately 60,000 churches and over 14,000 members. The CNBC member church conferences include the African Methodist Episcopal, Church of God in Christ, African Methodist Episcopal Zion, Christian Methodist Episcopal, National Baptist Convention of America, National Baptist Convention, U.S.A. Inc., and the Progressive National Baptist Convention, Inc.

CNBC is responsible for the historic 1984 agreement that for the first time forged a working coalition involving black churches and a major American industry. CNBC successfully negotiated the creation of a church-owned insurance agency with Aetna Life & Casualty Insurance Company and the black insurance management firm of Howard and Cloud of West Hartford, Connecticut. The organization and its member denominations own 70 percent of the newly created Church Insurance Partnership Agency (CIPA) with Aetna and Howard & Cloud as minority participants. CIPA will offer comprehensive casualty insurance for church properties and health, life, and annuity programs for the 250,000 employees of CNBC member denominations. In time, church members will be included in the program. "This marks the beginning of a new series of cooperative banking, purchasing, publishing, educational, and community development programs," said John Hurst Adams, AME Bishop and CNBC Chairman.

Soon to be launched in eight other cities, CNBC's cooperative banking program is now in operation in Washington, D.C. Twenty-five churches have funneled their monies to the black-owned United National Bank of Washington. According to CNBC executive director Joseph Eaglin, the average daily church balance is $28,000. The bank gets investment money and the church may realize from 6 to 12 percent yield from available funds. This money is used to expand or support other community ventures.

An important aspect of this program, Eaglin points out, is that the churches develop a strong relationship with the local bank, allowing for easier financing of church programs and the fostering of a partnership that will address the critical needs of the community. In addition, Eaglin discovered that the Washington project influenced local banks to maximize their efforts to concentrate funds within the black community.

The ultimate goal of the CNBC collective banking program is to develop a black church-owned financial corporation to serve as a vehicle for black economic development activities. The program, designed in cooperation with the Opportunity Funding Corporation, will set up a trust corporation that will be owned by the churches but closely connected to black banks. Its plan of action includes:

- Public meetings where church leaders raise the consciousness of their congregations to accept and develop financial plans.
- Visits to banks to demand the types of services and accounts the church's impressive resources can command.
- Forums where church leaders and community moderators develop strategies for assisting individual congregations in developing and implementing their financial programs.
- Meetings with black bank officials to encourage them to establish programs that might be tailored to the needs of churches.

A cash management system has also been devised that will increase the return on a church's finances. The objective of the system is to eliminate idle cash wherever possible. Checking and savings accounts are discouraged, while insured money fund accounts and money market or liquid accounts are encouraged.

The banking program, Eaglin explained, serves as the underpinning for purchasing and business development projects that will reduce overall church expenses, expand the capital base and allow for more support of local vendors and the creation of new businesses.

CNBC is now laying the groundwork for two ambitious undertakings: The Congress Press and the Black Church Cable TV Network. The Congress Press will be a profit-making umbrella structure for the six church-owned publishing houses currently operated by CNBC organizations. The Congress Press will open up church resources to provide outlets for talented black authors and artists who do not have access to traditional publishing sources.

The Black Church Cable TV Network will utilize untapped black community talent for its array of entertainment, educational, news, and information shows focused on the African-American Christian ethic.

A United House of Prayer

On its own, The United House of Prayer for All People (or The United House of Prayer, as it is more commonly known) has continued to blaze entrepreneurial trails as it did during the Depression years when its founder, Bishop C.M. (Daddy) Grace, led it into the manufacturing and distribution of commercial goods. The House of Prayer, which long ago evolved from a cult religion into a universally accepted and powerful Pentecostal organization, has always had a solid financial base because of its aggressive business activities. It is the home of Daddy Grace Toothpaste.

The House of Prayer is so rich and self-contained, it continues to prosper long after the death of its founder. This was not the case with Bishop Grace's arch rival, Father Divine. When Divine died, his empire crumbled. Today, under Bishop W. McCullough, The United House of Prayer, on the other hand, is the sole financier of all its projects and enterprises.

Its most ambitious program to date involves the construction of low-to-moderate-income housing in cities. With 146 churches in 22 states, it has drawn on its vast resources to invest $20 million in housing construction funds in three cities and will soon begin construction in eight others.

The House of Prayer, by design, purchases choice inner city property that is adjacent to newly renovated areas of the city. In Washington, D.C., the church, many years ago, bought a large parcel of land that had been devastated during the civil disturbances of the sixties. Today this area contains a still expanding (and wholly church-owned) housing development near the city's new convention center and adjacent to the new Metro subway system.

Bill Mitchell, a member of the church, was among the thousands of Washington, D.C., inner city blacks who were displaced from their homes when gentrification swept through the city. He was forced to move to a rural county in neighboring Maryland because he could no longer afford to rent or buy property in the city. Now he's back, with hundreds of others, as a resident in a new garden apartment complex in downtown Washington, D.C. The United House of Prayer puts up the money for its housing developments and subsidizes all rents as well. Maintaining a healthy, thriving black community in the city is all-important to the church.

"If it hadn't been for church housing, I could not afford to live in the city of Washington," said Mitchell.

A United House of Prayer spokesperson pointed out that church membership is not a qualification for residence in any of the church's housing developments.

"The idea is to build a better, stronger community by providing an affordable living base and decent housing," he said.

Every person or family is given individual rent consideration. Many pay even less than the far-below market rates that are quoted by the church as "average" rents for its properties. In Washington, D.C., where rent for a one-bedroom garden or terrace apartment will start at $450-$500, the United House of Prayer will charge $250; a two-bedroom will rent for $550 plus on the open market, the church will rent for $325.

"People respect our property because they know we respect them. There will be no inspectors or bureaucrats running through their place at all hours to check up on them; besides, in a very real sense, they know all this belongs to the collective 'us,' " said the church spokesperson.

Leaders Energizing Neighborhood Development (LEND)

Leaders Energizing Neighborhood Development (LEND) was founded in 1983 to harness the economic power of the black church and spur black community economic development.

Accordingly, LEND has divided up $1 million among ten

black churches around the country as seed money for the creation of community-based credit unions.

"These credit unions will serve as nerve centers, fostering other neighborhood development projects and stemming the negative outflow of savings from low-income neighborhoods," said Taft Holland, LEND President.

James Mosby, the volunteer administrator of the credit union project at Detroit's Hartford Memorial Baptist Church, is enthusiastic about the possibilities the program offers: "This is pure excitement to see the money reinvested in the community. We have big plans. We're now laying a strong foundation."

Although now primarily involved in consumer lending, Mosby said the church will soon move into the area of small business loans. Mosby, an economics professor at the University of Detroit, said his church, under activist pastor Charles A. Hill, has always pursued community empowerment strategies.

Recognizing that the black church develops a positive value orientation, by strengthening families and encouraging a communal sense of resource-sharing, LEND will tap into the network of community development activities that already fill the community church agenda.

With this base, LEND has started a computer learning center at Jones Tabernacle AME Church in Philadelphia. With other churches already designated as program participants, this pilot project has targeted youngsters in grades three to eight and, using more sophisticated techniques, those in grades nine to twelve.

A Neighborhood Approach

Vernon Dobson pastors Baltimore's Union Baptist Church in an aggressive, yet friendly, way. Dobson was one of the founders of the citywide interdenominational ministerial alliance that led to the formation of Baltimore United in Leadership Development (BUILD)—a still growing group of 32 churches committed to turning things around in Baltimore's low-income communities.

Union Baptist Church sits in the part of Baltimore once known as Sugar Hill where honky-tonks, sleazy bars, and bootleggers proliferated. As neighborhood residents prospered and married, they moved out of the area to the suburbs, joining the black middle class out-flight patterns of the fifties, sixties, and seventies. Those who fled to acquire space and property did not, however, give up their membership to Union Baptist. The neighborhood began to deteriorate noticeably though, as a combination, over the years, of landlord neglect, rising inner city unemployment, and bankrupt businesses clogged the community's lifelines.

Union Baptist responded by building "Greenwillow," a 143 unit low-income housing development to cope with an immediate housing crisis. It also invested in a coffee house and a neighborhood laundromat. The church is now in the process of renovating an entire block to create more low-income housing.

Union Baptist is also proud of its day care center. In operation since 1970, not only does it free community parents to take advantage of employment opportunities without having to worry about exorbitant child care fees, it serves as a job training vehicle for neighborhood residents.

"We have trained teacher aides, food service workers, bus drivers, clerical workers, and secretaries down through the years, placed them in jobs, strengthened their families, and made our community stronger," Dobson said.

BUILD and Dobson's last big campaign involved the hefty car insurance rates that were charged to inner city residents by insurance companies. BUILD pulled together a large research team from member churches that investigated accident statistics countrywide. Compiled information was broken down by race and by rural and city areas. Their conclusion:

Inner city residents have accidents at the same rate as those who live in rural areas. Armed with this information, BUILD revealed its findings to the local press, lobbied the city and state governments and sought out individual insurance companies to convince them that a ready, abundant market existed if rates were lowered so that more low-income residents could buy insurance policies.

The tactic worked. An insurance company was found that offered substantially reduced rates to residents of Baltimore's low-income neighborhoods. One hundred and fifty persons signed up immediately; those who had insurance previously, paid from $300-$500 less than what they had been paying.

Dobson views the black church as an "enabler" of the empowerment process. "The idea is to spin back profits into the community; the black church's role is to blend relationships so that mistrust and misunderstandings can be gotten rid of and the real job of living to one's fullest potential can begin."

Up the Street

Up the street from Union Baptist, at the corner, stands the 5,000 member Bethel AME Church, simply known as Bethel Baltimore. Boasting a synergetic relationship common to most black communities and a $600,000 annual budget, Bethel operates a bookstore, a thrift shop, a library, an employment agency, a credit union, a food co-op, a scholarship assistance program for youths and adults, an in-school tutoring program, a full-scale adult education program, and the Henry McLauren Academy of Learning where regularly scheduled courses are held in financial planning and family budgeting.

"A minimum wage reduced by food and rent leaves very little for savings," explained Leonidas Fowlkes, manager of Bethel's credit union. Add this to the fact that banks turn away small depositors and "you got a problem," he said.

Bethel responded to this dilemma in 1979 by forming a credit union that offered shares for a nominal $5.25 to anyone in the community who wished to join. Capitalized at $93,000 by the church congregation, the 600-member Bethel Credit Union has set up payroll deduction programs at several area nursing homes, launched a mutual fund investment program, and sponsored workshops and courses on investing, planning, and budgeting.

"Financial education in a low-income area is a link-up process that stresses discipline and application; that's the beauty of it, it's goal-oriented and it works," said Fowlkes.

"Our churches work together with a common goal in mind; we pool our information and share our resources for the betterment of the whole community."

Bethel AME, at 200 years old, is an excellent example of a church that has kept apace of its community during changing times. Like Union Baptist, its doors stay open seven days a week to allow community residents the space and resources to take control of their individual lives. In this way, a chronologically old church remains young and vigorous.

The Action Agenda

Economic development has long been an important function of the black church. Since the sixties, however, it has adopted more and more of the practices of Big Business. Economic diversity with an emphasis on black community reinvestment is the black church clarion call of the eighties. The interdenominational national conference alliances represent a giant leap toward community empowerment and self-reliance. The prospect of billion dollar organizations working toward a common goal augurs well for those people outside the U.S. economic mainstream.

Equally inspired are the programs being developed by individual churches or small clusters of churches. The "we can do that, too" syndrome is typified by the Reverend C. L. Long's Scripture Church of Our Lord Jesus Christ, which co-sponsors and promotes gospel concerts along with Washington, D.C.'s black-owned radio station, WYCB. In the eighties, with creativity and relevance, the black church, both locally and nationally, has seized, with zest, the initiative for turning the black community around economically.

The church, by tradition, is a self-starter preferring to carry out its own agenda by using its own resources. The vagaries of government policy have never had any major influence on project timetables. In fact, some pastors who accepted minimal government funds now have regrets about doing even that. The heft, the feel, of doing it alone and doing it better has always had an immense appeal among the black church leadership.

The black church is now determined to bail out the low-income, economically stagnant black communities of the land. Its traditional value system coupled with a contemporary agenda has sparked fire and enthusiasm in the breasts of that community's old and young. Its membership is again on the rise.

Church, Employee, and Member Breakdown
Of Major Black Denominations

AFRICAN METHODIST EPISCOPAL	2,700,000	Members
5,500 Churches	14,350	Employees
AFRICAN METHODIST EPISCOPAL		
ZION	1,500,000	Members
3,200 Churches	7,895	Employees
CHRISTIAN METHODIST EPISCOPAL	753,000	Members
1,763 Churches	4,183	Employees
CHURCH OF GOD IN CHRIST	3,500,000	Members
8,250 Churches	16,000	Employees
NATIONAL BAPTIST CONVENTION,		
U.S.A, INC.	6,000,000	Members
27,000 Churches	68,000	Employees
NATIONAL BAPTIST CONVENTION		
OF AMERICA	3,000,000	Members
11,300 Churches	22,000	Employees
PROGRESSIVE NATIONAL BAPTIST		
CONVENTION, INC.	1,200,000	Members
2,000 Churches	5,350	Employees

The Black Family: Building on Strengths

BY ROBERT B. HILL

Black families are currently in the throes of a social and economic crisis of unprecedented dimensions. Between 1970 and 1983, the unemployment rate for all blacks soared from 8 percent to 20 percent—the highest level ever recorded for blacks by the U.S. Labor Department. During that same period, poverty among blacks climbed from 30 percent to 36 percent—one of the highest rates for blacks since the early 1960s. These economic dislocations, because of back-to-back recessions and double-digit inflation, severely undermined the social fabric of black families.

Each percentage increase in black unemployment has led to a comparable rise in one-parent families, pushing the proportion of black families headed by women from 28 to 42 percent between 1970 and 1983. Moreover, over half of all black births today are out-of-wedlock compared to about 25 percent 20 years ago. Although the circumstances of whites also worsened, the economic gap between blacks and whites is greater today than it was over a decade ago.

The failure of the billions of dollars spent in social services programs to make inroads into minority unemployment and poverty has convinced many observers that the problems of black families are unsolvable. But these seemingly unsolvable problems *do* have solutions.

The last twenty years have yielded new insights into how to create effective programs to aid minority and poor families. Unfortunately, this new knowledge of workable family-strengthening strategies has not been incorporated into the national dialogue about black families. Moreover, thousands of community-based groups throughout the nation are demonstrating every day that it is possible to help black and low-income families to effectively resolve such problems as unemployment, poverty, welfare dependence, adolescent pregnancy, poor academic performance, delinquency, and crime. Yet these *successful* inner city efforts are unknown to the vast majority of policymakers and practitioners. Consequently, the American public's understanding of the black family dynamic has not progressed over the last two decades.

A Narrow View

This widespread ignorance results mainly from the fact that the news media, many policymakers, and social scientists employ a "blame the victim" perspective that suffers from three fundamental flaws:

(a) It attributes most problems of black families to internal deficiencies.

(b) It fails to incorporate numerous new research findings about black and poor families.

(c) It fails to focus on successful models or strategies for resolving some of the problems identified.

According to this way of thinking, higher rates of black unemployment result from a lack of education, job skills, and a proper work ethic and *not* because of discrimination, periodic recessions, or technological advances that influence the job market.

This blame-the-victim attitude is characterized by the following practices:

- *Monolithic treatment of black families based on family structure.* One-parent families are described as if all of them are poor, on welfare, and have low-achieving children, while two-parent families are portrayed as if none of them are poor, on welfare, or have low-achieving children.
- *A preoccupation with unrepresentative segments of black families.* For example, the news media concentrates its greatest attention on poor, one-parent families on welfare, who comprise only 15 percent of all black families.
- *Unbalanced analyses that focus exclusively on the weaknesses of black families without any examination of their positive attributes.* For example, the contemporary contributions of extended family networks (uncles, aunts, grandmothers, etc.) are de-emphasized or totally ignored.
- *Static analyses that ignore downward mobility among the "middle class" and upward mobility among the "working class" and "underclass."* The constant up and down movement of middle class persons who lose their jobs and sink into a low-income category coupled with people who rise economically from the underclass are not reflected in social scientists' evaluations.
- *Omission of research data that contradict basic assumptions of the blame-the-victim syndrome.* For example, studies that reveal high turnover rates among welfare and low-income groups are usually ignored in favor of portraying blacks as stagnated individuals on welfare rolls.
- *Using double standards in analyses of black and white families.* Single parent families among blacks and low-income groups are described as "pathological" structures headed by

73

"matriarchs," while one-parent families among white and middle-income groups are described as "alternative lifestyles" headed by "supermoms."

Over the past two decades, this type of thinking has been the dominant perspective of the news media in its analyses of black families. In late 1983, *The New York Times* presented a series on *the* black family, which focused almost solely on poor one-parent families on welfare—a group comprising one out of six black families and less than one-third of all single-parent black families. In December 1984, Baltimore's *Evening Sun* ran a series on black families that was so stereotyped that the black community launched a boycott of the newspaper. Many social scientists—both black and white—use this same narrow view in their studies of blacks in America as well.

Finding Solutions

Two basic premises underpin effective family support strategies: (a) families need to build on their existing strengths, and (b) they need to focus on what they can do to help themselves.

What *are* the strengths of families? Family strengths are traits that enhance the ability of the family to meet the needs of its members and the demands made on it by systems outside the family. The following five strengths have been especially functional for the survival, stability, and advancement of black families.

(a) Strong work orientation

(b) Flexibility of family roles

(c) Strong achievement orientation

(d) Extended family networks

(e) Strong religious orientation

Although these characteristics can be found among other groups, they have manifested themselves differently in black families because of the unique history of slavery and other forms of racial oppression experienced by blacks in America.

Work Orientation

Numerous studies have revealed that the overwhelming majority of low-income and middle-income blacks have a strong work commitment and prefer self-reliance to welfare dependence. About 70 percent of the heads of all black families are currently in the official labor force (they are either working or actively looking for work). [12] Adding the discouraged workers (those who want to work but have become too discouraged to look) would raise the actual labor force participation rate of black family heads to about 80 percent.

Contrary to popular belief, heads of single-parent black families are more work-oriented today than they were a decade ago. Between 1969 and 1981, the proportion of female family heads in the official labor force jumped from 50 percent to 60 percent. Unfortunately, these labor force rates are not fully translated into jobs, since only 60 percent of all black family heads and about half of all female family heads are currently employed. When the discouraged workers are included—as is done in the National Urban League's Hidden Unemployment Index—the actual jobless rate for black adults in 1983 was 29 percent, one and a half times higher than their official rate (17%).[13]

But the subgroup in black families that experienced the sharpest decline in employment over the past decade was young people. Between 1969 and 1983, the proportion of black 16 to 19-year-olds in the official labor force fell from 40 percent to 35 percent. Over the same period, their official jobless rate doubled from 24 percent to 49 percent. And, when discouraged youthful workers are added, the actual jobless rate for black teenagers in 1983 was an astronomical 69 percent. Some observers attribute the persistently high jobless rates among black youth to lack of education. But while educational deficiencies are clearly important factors, they cannot fully account for these alarming rates; particularly when white high school dropouts have a lower jobless rate (24%) than blacks who have completed high school (38%) and about the same rate as blacks who have gone to college (25%).[14]

Grassroots Remedies

These depression-level jobless rates among black adults and youth have inspired aggressive community-based employment and training initiatives across the nation. For 75 years, the National Urban League has provided a broad range of employability services to blacks through its community-based affiliates. Similarly, since the 1960s, the Reverend Leon Sullivan's Opportunities Industrialization Centers (OIC) have provided job training services to blacks both here and abroad. However, as U.S. Labor Department funding guidelines placed increased emphasis on the quantity rather than the quality of services, the inevitable "creaming" of clients—the sifting out of the most skilled for training slots—resulted in increasing numbers of the hard-core unskilled being left out by the major government-funded manpower programs.

In an effort to reach this group, several successful community programs emerged that were specifically targeted to these hard-core unemployables. The Youth Enterprise Society (SAY YES) in Los Angeles, California, and Youth-in-Action in Chester, Pennsylvania, are among the community agencies that successfully combated gang violence and drug addiction by providing meaningful employment opportunities for troubled youth.[15]

76

Several innovative grassroots efforts were also developed to reduce welfare dependency. Since the 1960s, some of the most effective programs have emanated from the resident management corporations of public housing developments now represented in over 15 cities. These groups have demonstrated that public housing residents can operate and manage a development more efficiently and cost effectively than local housing authorities. More importantly, they have demonstrated that welfare dependency can be reduced by creating businesses and jobs for their fellow residents.

Operation Life, founded by former welfare recipient Ruby Duncan, is another community-based development corporation that has increased business and employment opportunities for the hard-core unemployed among blacks in Las Vegas, Nevada. Also, the Dade Women's Welfare Coalition is developing day care centers and food cooperatives in order to enhance employment options for welfare recipients in Miami, Florida. The Nationwide Work Experiment, funded by the federal government, has also demonstrated that the employability of long-term welfare recipients can be improved through effective community-based services.

Flexibility of Family Roles

Most American families experienced a greater flexibiity and interchanging of roles during the 1970s because of such factors as periodic recessions and increased numbers of women joining the work force. This resulted in mothers assuming some of the traditional roles of fathers, fathers performing some of the traditional functions of mothers, and children performing some parental functions. This increased role flexibiity and adaptability was most evident in the growth of families headed by women who were the primary breadwinners of their households.

Traditionally, families headed by women are depicted as "broken," "discouraged," or "pathological," while two-parent families are characterized as "intact," "cohesive," and "healthy." However, many research studies have revealed that two parents do not make a family intact any more than having one parent makes it a broken family. The incidence of child runaways, for example, is greatest in so-called "intact" two-parent families located in the inner city. Recent statistics on child abuse, battered wives, and incest reveal a higher prevalence of family violence in "intact" two-parent suburban families than is commonly believed. The actual extent of cohesion in many two-parent families is highly questionable, as one out of two of them ends in divorce or separation. In fact, female-headed families increased among whites just as fast as they did among blacks during the 1970s.

Many white families are now attempting to adopt the flexibility that has been traditionally characteristic of black families, particularly regarding the sharing of household chores. Contrary to popular belief, two-parent black families have been distinguished by equalitarian, rather than matriarchal, role responsibilities. That is, husbands in black families are more likely to share various role responsibilities (such as cooking, taking out the garbage, disciplining children, etc.) than husbands in white families.

However, one trend toward increasing role flexibility in black families has been very alarming—the high number of out-of-wedlock births among adolescents. Youngsters, who can be categorized as children themselves, must assume the non-traditional roles of parent and breadwinner. Although the illegitimacy rate has been steadily declining among black teenagers while rising among white teenagers, black teenagers are still five times more likely than white teenagers to have babies out-of-wedlock. An added complication is that babies born to adolescents have a higher risk of low birth weight, poor nutrition, and mortality than babies born to adults.

Many community-based efforts have been launched in inner cities across the nation to advise and counsel both single adult parent families and those headed by unwed adolescent parents. For more than a decade, the Sisterhood of Black Single Mothers (founded by Daphne Busby in the Bedford-Stuyvesant section of Brooklyn, New York) has demonstrated that it is possible to improve the social and economic well-being of teenage mothers by teaching them to place a value on self-worth, parenting skills, and educational attainment. Because of its effectiveness with young mothers, this group has formed an off-shoot group of young males to strengthen parental responsibility among adolescent fathers.

Examples of other community-based groups that provide a broad array of supportive services to single mothers include: the Webster Avenue Resource Center (Rochester, New York), Pryde (Pittsburgh, Pennsylvania), Family Dynamics (Brooklyn, New York), the Teenage Pregnancy and Parenting Program (San Francisco, California), and local chapters of the Delta Sigma Theta sorority. Special programs targeted to black adolescent fathers were also being conducted by local chapters of the Alpha Phi Alpha fraternity, Concerned Black Men, the National Urban League, and many neighborhood-based groups and organizations.

Achievement Orientation

The strong achievement orientation in black families was evident in the sharp increase in high school graduation and college enrollment among black youth during the 1970s. As the proportion of high school dropouts among black youth, 16 to 24-years-old, decreased from 41 percent to 31 percent between 1971 and 1983, the proportion of black youth graduating from high school rose from 48 percent to 52 percent.[16] In 1977, about the same proportion of black (50%) and white (51%) high school graduates went to college. (However, by 1983, the number of black high school graduates going to college plummeted to 39 percent while their white counterparts jumped to 55 percent.[17] Loss of student grants and high unemployment were factors.)

Black colleges continue to be a major lifeline for thousands of black students. Although only one-fifth of all black college students attend historically black institutions today, these colleges account for two-fifths of all baccalaureate degrees conferred on blacks.[18] This disproportionate allotment of degrees by black colleges results from their high student retention rate. About 70 percent of all blacks in predominantly black institutions complete their courses of study, while about 70 percent of blacks attending predominantly white colleges do not graduate.[19] A comprehensive study of black college students by Jacqueline Fleming reveals that blacks in black colleges often show greater improvement in academic performance, social adjustment, self-concept, and identity than those attending white colleges.[20]

The strong achievement orientation of black youth is just as prevalent in one-parent as two-parent families. Contrary to patterns among white youth, black youth from one-parent families are just as likely to go to college as youth from two-parent families. Many community-based education programs in inner city areas are designed to reinforce the strong achievement ethic in black families.

Without a doubt, Head Start is the largest community-based pre-school program for minority and low-income children in the country. However, the 400,000 children served by this federal government-sponsored program in 1980 comprised only 20 percent of all children eligible for its services. Although most evaluations of Head Start indicate that this program has been effective in improving the child's attainment in first grade, the program's impact diminishes substantially as the child moves through subsequent grades. Consequently, many black parents feel the need for alternative educational institutions.

There are now over 250 neighborhood-based, independent schools across the nation that attempt to give low-income black parents the same option of quality education in the private sector available to middle and upper-income parents. Some of these schools are: the Lower East Side International Community School (New York) where children are introduced to computers and second languages at the age of four; the W.E.B. Du Bois Academic Institute (Los Angeles); the Red School House (St. Paul); the Sheenway School and Cultural Center (Los Angeles); and Randal Hyland (Washington, D.C.). Some of the schools are spin-offs of the Street Academy (Baltimore). These independent schools provide an impressive educational option at nominal cost to low-income children from pre-schoolers through high school.

As the late Ron Edmond's study of effective schools revealed, quality education can be provided to low-income students in public schools where there is strong and dedicated leadership and a caring faculty. Many public schools across the nation exist as islands of excellence, but more are needed.

Extended Family Networks

One of the most important sources of strength among black families over the past decade has been the extended family network. According to conventional wisdom, the extended family is supposed to be virtually extinct in urban areas today. On the contrary, black families experienced a strong revival of the extended family during the 1970s.

Periodic recessions were responsible for increases in "doubling up" or the moving in of families (particularly those headed by single mothers) with relatives. The devastating 1974–75 recession caused the proportion of black children living with their mothers in households of kin to soar from 30 percent to 39 percent between 1973 and 1975.[21]

The increase in out-of-wedlock births among black teenagers also contributed to a growth in extended family households, as 85 percent of the children born to single black teenagers live in the households of their grandparents. Grandmothers in the contemporary extended families are much younger (35 to 45-years-old) than those of a decade ago (55 to 65-years-old).

Kinship networks are also called on increasingly to provide affordable, quality day care services for working parents. About half of all black working mothers who need child care depend on relatives for such services, 20 percent use nonrelatives (especially neighbors and friends), while only five percent use day care centers. Single mothers rely on kin for day care much more than women living with their husbands. Some 83 percent of black women who were never married use relatives for day care, compared to 41 percent of black women who are currently married.[22]

In addition to providing informal services in such areas as day care, foster care, adoption, and adolescent pregnancy, extended families also play a major role in reducing child abuse. Research studies have consistently found the highest rates of child abuse among parents who are isolated from kin and the lowest rates among parents who are integral parts of a cohesive kinship network.

Informal adoption and foster care, the historic service of extended families, was provided increasingly during the 1970s. Between 1970 and 1979, the number of informally adopted black children living with relatives (usually the grandparents or aunts and uncles) went from 1.3 million to 1.4 million, causing the proportion of all black children living in informal adoptive households to jump from 13 percent to 15 percent. Interestingly, female-headed black families are three times (37%) more likely than husband-wife families (12%) to informally adopt children.[23]

Black families informally adopt ten times more children than are placed through formal adoptive agencies. Yet many agencies continue to claim that black families do not adopt children. On the contrary, according to a nationwide survey of black households conducted in 1981, two-fifths (37%) of all black families are interested in taking in a foster child, while 30 percent are interested in legally adopting one.[24] Some three million black families indicated their interest in adopting black children. These families could easily absorb four times the number of black children that are born out-of-wedlock each year.

These statistics become especially important when serious consideration is given to changing this country's publicly supported $2 billion a year foster care system. Nearly half the approximately 275,000 children locked in this system are black. Social welfare industry officials continue to attribute the high number of blacks or "special needs" children caught in this bureaucratic web to both the alleged unwillingness of black families to adopt and the high teenage birth rate.

The real villain, however, is the snarl of red tape and tangle of rules, regulations, and adoption procedures that screen out many black families interested in adoption. Those who dominate the selection and placement process often apply inappropriate standards in evaluating the qualifications of blacks to care for children. For example, most white agencies automatically rule out single parents, older persons, and low-income parents—the foundations of the black extended family network.

The current system has evolved into an industry with perverse incentives for social agencies to keep children because

83

these children bring increased revenue. Some 70 percent of the money allocated for the nation's foster care program is spent for administrative overhead and services. ·

Detroit's Homes for Black Children (HBC) founded over a decade ago by a young black social worker named Sydney Duncan, is an example of a successful, independent, community-based adoption agency that, with ease, finds adoptive homes for so-called "hard-to-place" foster care children. In its first year, HBC placed 137 children, compared to 96 placed by the combined efforts of 13 traditional agencies.

Other innovative adoption agencies that place black foster children include: Akiba (Akron, Ohio), Black Family Outreach (Little Rock, Arkansas), Harlem-Dowling Children's Service (New York City), Medina Children's Service (Seattle, Washington), and Spaulding for Children (Kansas, New York, and Ohio).

Many of these groups have used the extended family approach to prevent the unnecessary placement of black children in foster care. The assumption of these agencies, put simply, is that an adoptable child *can* be placed in the black community. The high placement rate stems, in large part, from this premise.

Many of these groups have used the extended family approach to prevent the unnecessary placement of black children in foster care. The agency, through its supportive services, becomes a part of the extended family network by initiating regular contact with the parents and children of multi-problem families. Homes for Black Children, for instance, operates a Family Preservation Program whose sole purpose is to keep a family intact and functioning as a unit. Similarly, the Lower Eastside Family Union (New York City) and Harlem's Hale House have also prevented the unnecessary foster care placement of scores of babies born to mothers who were addicted to drugs, alcoholic, or incarcerated; in effect, serving as a surrogate grandmother to them. Special counseling, nutrition programs, and tutorial projects are some of the methods used to weld a family bond.

Some of the most effective family support groups in inner cities have been those that have reinforced existing extended family networks or developed surrogate extended families where none existed previously. The House of Umoja, founded by Sister Falaka Fattah, used the African extended family model to successfully reduce gang violence and delinquency among troubled black youth in Philadelphia. Counseling, peer group discussions, and shared activities were regular exercises that cemented relationships by cooling down hostilities and anxieties.

Sister Fattah also pioneered a group house concept, with a central authority figure, that designated areas of responsibility for each inhabitant. The results were so dramatic that Philadelphia's criminal justice system tapped into the resources of the House of Umoja by referring delinquents directly there rather than isolating them in area reform schools and detention centers.

For those unlucky enough to have spent most, or all, of their youth in the foster care system, community-based groups such as Freedom Through Choices (Washington, D.C.) and Harlem Interfaith Counseling Service exist to facilitate the transition to independent living. Job training and placement programs and surrogate extended family concepts are used to aid troubled adolescents who have spent most of their lives in this institutional limbo.

Black leaders and other policymakers earnestly seeking effective ways to aid black families to meet the challenges of the day must first seek solutions that already exist within the social fabric of the black community. Rather than expanding government social welfare policies and programs that often exacerbate the very problems they were designed to solve, policy-makers and others need to eliminate the barriers to continued black family growth and prosperity.

Religious Orientation

The most important strength of black families, according to many black people, is their strong religious commitment. In fact, blacks are more likely than whites to feel that religion plays a major role in their lives. According to a 1981 Gallup survey, 67 percent of blacks said that religion was "very important" in their lives, compared to only 55 percent of whites. Moreover, the overwhelming majority of blacks belong to churches and attend them regularly. Based on the National Urban League's Black Pulse Survey of 1979–80, three-fourths (76%) of all blacks belong to churches and two-thirds (67%) attend them at least once a month, while about half (48%) attend them weekly. Furthermore, 71 percent of all black parents send their children to Sunday School regularly. And there is some evidence that blacks reared in the church have higher educational and occupational attainment than those without religious upbringing.

Most of the denominations reported a rise in membership over the past decade. Some observers attribute this increase to record-level unemployment and inflation, as church membership traditionally rises during economic recessions and declines during periods of recovery. However, other commentators give some credit to the resurgence of social activism among black churches. As the most independent and self-sufficient institution in the black community, the black church has been a major source of strength, stability, and advancement for blacks since slavery.

Government cutbacks in funds for social programs induced many black churches to assume their historic role as a support for extended families. Thus, black churches have significantly enhanced their family strengthening efforts. For example, Family Life Centers, such as the one established by the Shiloh Baptist Church in Washington, D.C., are being replicated across the nation in order to apply an holistic approach to meeting the needs of low-income and middle-income families. Similarly, many denominations have formed Quality Life Centers and have set up a wide range of programs to enhance parenting skills, educational achievement, marital stability, positive male-female relations, and the adoption of "hard-to-place" children.

The Action Agenda

New data on the black family coupled with the innovative nature of community-based self-help programs are contributing solutions to socioeconomic problems that threaten to overwhelm minority and low-income family units.

At present, many of the public social welfare policies and programs intended to assist black families are, in fact, undermining them. These programs, mired in a self-defeating blame-the-victim bias, are not only doomed to failure but, in many instances, actually exacerbate the new problems they were designed to alleviate.

Social scientists, policymakers, and the news media must all undergo a reorientation in thinking that allows a fuller understanding of the black family dynamic. These various elements of the public policy-making process should be made aware of the effective programs that have been generated by community-based groups for dealing with the problems of minority and low-income families.

Grassroots self-help programs demonstrate each day that it is possible to make inroads into unemployment, poverty, welfare dependency, adolescent pregnancy, poor academic performance, delinquency, and crime. These largely unheralded efforts, which build on existing family strengths, rather than weaknesses, should serve as the standard by which all new programs are measured.

There is now ample evidence to indicate that when the black community mobilizes its own internal resources, establishes its own standards, and employs its own unique and innovative approaches, forces are put into motion that strengthen and reinforce it.

CASE STUDY #2:

HOMES FOR BLACK CHILDREN

A Haven in the Bureaucratic Storm

Sydney Duncan, president of Detroit's Homes for Black Children (HBC), has become an acknowledged pioneer in the field of foster care and adoption. Duncan has embellished the concept of the black extended family with such success that her young agency's minority placement record exceeds the combined total minority placement rate of Detroit's other adoption agencies. HBC's innovative techniques, keyed to a basic knowledge of the black family structure, have allowed it to place over 800 children since the agency began operating in 1969.

Duncan, a former social worker, is aware of the fact that the $2 billion-a-year foster care system has evolved into an industry of perverse incentives. Studies have shown that some 70 percent of the money allotted for foster care nationwide is spent on overhead and salaries. It has been reported that one agency, for example, receives $24,000 a year for each child in its care, but spends less than $3.00 a day to feed and clothe each child. In another documented instance, four agencies in the same city received a total of $6 million to place 2,000 children, yet among them, only ten children were placed after a year's time.

Duncan cites these examples of bureaucratic ineptitude and greed as the primary reason why some 105,000 black children are "trapped" in the foster care system. Even more damage is done to these young people when, upon their release at age 18, a disproportionately high number of minority youth wind up in jails and mental hospitals because there are no programs to prepare them for a positive adjustment to society. Many foster care "refugees" are arrested on vagrancy charges because they were not taught job skills or proper work habits while in the system.

In addition, great numbers of children are trapped in the system because the issue of parental rights has not been adjudicated. Foot-dragging and non-action on the part of agencies on this issue has guaranteed them a steady pool of "clients" while huge monetary outlays for services have perpetuated employment for those who are a part of the social welfare industry.

Homes for Black Children, by contrast, has demonstrated that the real interests of children need not be sacrificed to the money-making, self-serving interests of the foster care system. Rather than get bogged down in so-called "traditional" approaches, the HBC staff aggressively recruits families, places a premium on handling inquiries with sensitivity and patience, and makes certain that there always exists a mutual respect between case workers and prospective parents.

The HBC staff has exploded the myth that black parents do not adopt by introducing other innovative techniques. Although many agencies may charge as much as $5,000 for child placement, HBC does not charge a fee. HBC makes use of the black extended family concept by placing children in single-parent households and deliberately seeking out households with "aunts," "uncles," or "grandparent" figures. These heads-of-households symbolically represent the blood relatives who, for generations, have reared children who were not their own.

HBC has also dramatically reduced the "home study" time from a national average of two years to just under six months. This time represents the period agency personnel spend in evaluating the suitability of a household as a home for an adopted child. Duncan explained that the shortening of this process has resulted in keeping the interest of prospective adopting families keen and alive. HBC also slashes through bureaucratic red tape (and saves a considerable amount of time and money) by providing adopting families with facsimile birth certificates when originals cannot be found. Duncan has repeatedly emphasized, and has the track record to prove, that high placement rates can be achieved by a simple "speeding up" of the entire adoptive process.

To serve the community better, Duncan has drawn up a set of four principles that account for the success of her agency.

- Homes for Black Children sees its task, not as a job, but a "cause"—it is important to define *what* is to be done and *for whom* specifically. Success is measured in terms of *product* (the number of children placed), not process (that is, the number of work hours spent, tests given, or some other "professional" activity engaged in).
- The staff does not have preconceptions regarding a prospective parent's politics, lifestyle, or "type" of adoptive home. The applicant's capacity to love and care for a child is regarded as most relevant. The staff is accountable only to the children and refuses to be shackled by institutionalized and administrative barriers.
- Instead of focusing on statistical abstractions about a need for black adoptions, Homes for Black Children transposes statistics into specific living children by placing the pictures and stories of these children on television and in the Detroit papers. Instead of public service announcements that accost the community with the "burden" of hard-to-place or special-needs children, the pictures show the joy experienced by Detroit's black families who have achieved parental satisfaction. Instead of discussing racism or poverty, the announcements stress tranquility and the idea of giving children homes where they can find love, food, and a place to live in peace.
- As the needs for adoption change, Homes for Black Children changes its program. After a year and a half of operation, so many black infants had been placed that there was a waiting list

of families wishing to adopt. HBC accordingly began to focus more on the placement of older and "retarded" children. When other agencies in Detroit realized that HBC was outperforming them, they altered their practices, as well.

Replication of the HBC model in other cities has produced dramatic results. Homes for Black Children in Phoenix, Arizona, had nearly 30 black families on its waiting list one month after it opened for registration. The Washington, D.C., Homes for Black Children program has also experienced a high placement rate.

The black community has developed solutions that could substantially reduce the number of black children in foster care. These innovative, neighborhood-based adoption programs and solutions for special needs children should be promoted and adapted nationwide.

F I V E

Education and Learning: Feeding the Hunger

BY ROBERT L. WOODSON

From the beginning of the black American experience, the quest for education has been insatiable. Following emancipation, an educational explosion spanning eighty years nearly wiped out black illiteracy.

Education and literacy, always highly prized by black America, were especially valued during slavery because the ability to read and write was associated with freedom. Brutal reprisals be damned! Books were sneaked onto plantations, hoarded, and protected like gold bars, and the business of learning was tended to in stealthy fashion.

One of the first end runs around obstacles to achieve an education occurred in 1803 when Prince Hall, a free black, opened the first black independent school in his Boston home. Hall's efforts, prompted by low black attendance in a hostile public school system, was an immediate success that launched similar schools in other cities and towns. His example lives today in over 200 independent community-based schools operating nationwide that serve as a stimulating alternative to the many moribund institutions posing as schools today.

It is significant that the earliest examples of black learning were initiated by the black community itself. Black entrepreneurs and professionals along with the black church and fraternal organizations joined together to provide schooling, legally or illegally, in every state that had a significant black presence.

To meet the demands of four million newly freed, education-starved blacks, a variety of resources were pressed into service. Northern teachers and missionary societies, both black and white, joined with the short-lived Freedmen's Bureau in establishing "Freedom Schools" to educate the black masses.

Often a clash would develop between black-controlled and white-sponsored schools in the same locale. The dispute would invariably involve northern white missionaries trying to gain control over black-initiated, self-help programs. After going up against the black-controlled Savannah Education Association of Savannah, Georgia, in 1865, a white missionary wrote the American Missionary Association (AMA) that "they have a natural praiseworthy pride in keeping their educational institutions in their own hands. There is jealousy of the superintendence of the white man in this matter. What they desire is assistance without control."[25]

Those being taught also made a distinction. Although grateful for any pathway to literacy, the new pupils clearly preferred black instruction. One missionary complained to the AMA: "Many parents prefer to send their children to colored teachers and pay a dollar a month for tuition than to send them to our schools free."[26]

Advancement and self-determination were the principal motivations behind the black onslaught on the schoolhouse door. But labor unions and worker organizations were unyielding in their efforts to close off avenues for those educated blacks who sought economic advancement. In fact, unions would aggressively bust up an enterprise started by blacks (catering, for example) by organizing a whites-only membership that would effectively coerce the predominantly white community into patronizing the newly formed white businesses. Blacks who got there first with the goods were often dealt this crushing blow.

The opposition of white skilled craftsmen, industrial and agricultural workers, and other labor organizations did not stifle the black urge to learn, however. These acts coupled with decreased public expenditures for black public education and stiff "literacy tests" for potential black voters only intensified black America's craving for knowledge. As if to underscore this determination, the black illiteracy rate dropped from 70 to 30 percent between 1880 and 1910—a period when disenfranchisement, terrorism, and Jim Crow were at their peak.

Leadership

Wilberforce University, one of the first black colleges, was opened in 1856 by the African Methodist Episcopal Church. It was concerned then, as it is now, with nurturing and developing black leadership capabilities—an avowed purpose of the Wilberforce counterparts sponsored by the other black church denominations. The African Methodist Episcopal Zion Church, the Christian Methodist Episcopal Church, and the Baptists all played a part in creating educational opportunities for black America.

Great minds like that of W.E.B. Du Bois were attracted by the atmosphere of commitment present at colleges like Wilberforce, so it was there that he accepted his first teaching post and, in effect, launched his brilliant career as educator, social scientist, writer, and editor.

Du Bois issued a report to a black educational conference in 1901 that documented the financial expenditures for black and white public schools in 16 southern states and Washington,

D.C., and made even more remarkable the amazing drop in the black illiteracy rate. The study pointed out that in Mississippi, for example, blacks were 60 percent of the school-age population in 1899, but received less than 20 percent of school expenditures—far less than the sum black Mississippians paid for state, county, and city taxes. Furthermore, the school year lasted only 101 days, or less than four months. It was the black community that stepped into the breach, with its "back-up" educational support systems, and prevented the public school system from turning out generations of functioning illiterates.

Other voices besides Du Bois were heard in the land. At Alabama's Tuskegee Institute, founder Booker T. Washington was calling for a "Negro industrial education" that consisted of literacy training, handyman crafts, and manual labor. Washington, compromised by the fact that Tuskegee was a state land-grant institution, was wholly committed to a black educational system that did not conflict with white supremacist values. This was the only way, he thought, that blacks, fresh from slavery, could be absorbed into the prevailing southern white-supremacist socioeconomic system. The black educator's reasoning, however, was clearly out of step with the thinking of black people at-large. They wanted quality education that allowed them to compete with whites for job positions.

According to studies, testimony given at congressional hearings, and special education reports, blacks preferred separate but *equal* educational facilities. Integration was hardly an issue as this debate raged in the late 1800s. The issue was whether blacks should pursue a quality education that developed skills—an education that included law schools, medical schools, and institutes of technology, or whether blacks should settle for "Negro industrial education." In short order, black institutions such as Howard, Fisk, and Meharry Medical

College beefed up their standards and expanded their schools to reflect the majority attitude. To further do battle with Washington's education philosophy of grabbing the lowest rung, southern blacks would soon begin the Great Migration to the North where they would engage in toe-to-toe combat with labor unions over securing skilled job positions. Washington's sudden death prevented his seeing a mass repudiation of many of his views.

Public Education No Panacea

Jim Crow public education, whether by statute in the South or *de facto* in the North, operated with an inspired cadre of black teachers. Many were frustrated engineers, doctors, lawyers, and architects, who synthesized this emotion into positive classroom energy that willed, as well as taught, the academic disciplines needed to succeed. Black teachers knew, by rote, how to fuse toughness with tenderness, and concern with objectivity, to shake and cajole the best out of their charges.

Black teachers worked for 10 to 50 percent less than their white counterparts and often taught two different grades sitting side-by-side in one classroom. Their achievement in turning out black students capable of coping with every aspect of American life is legendary.

This teaching zeal was a mission of race; it was certainly not a mandate from a deliberately underfunded black public school system that offered the bare bones of dilapidated buildings, outdated textbooks, and leftover supplies from the white system. In many areas, blacks were double-taxed because they wholly financed the purchase of school sites, school houses, and school furniture in order to secure a quality education for their children while still supporting their state's segregated system.

As the black population in urban areas swelled, no attempt was made in most cities to improve or expand facilities to accommodate the influx. Coincidentally, black graduates of secondary schools who wished to continue their education could not all be absorbed by the black college network. These factors, during the 1920s, 1930s, and 1940s, caused the great internal push for black education to run into a wall. The black craving for education had overwhelmed both good and bad intentions. Black community resources could not keep pace with the hunger for knowledge, on the one hand, while Jim Crow statutes and policies refused to surrender ground on the other. Something had to give.

The statistics told the story. In 1947, there still did not exist an institution in the South where a black could pursue studies for a doctorate. Howard, America's largest black university, had 7,000 enrolled students during that year but, if it had been physically possible, three or four times that number *could* have been accepted. That same year, its pharmacy and dentistry schools could accept only 50 students each, though more than ten times that number had submitted applications that qualified them for admittance.

Positions began to shift in black America regarding integrated education. Knowing that separate but equal facilities should never have been the law of the land, civil rights organizations—notably the NAACP—began testing the courts to see whether blacks could tap into the abundance of white education facilities.

By the time the landmark 1954 Supreme Court decision in *Brown v. Board of Education* brought an end to legal segregation in this country, years of neglect, gerrymandered housing patterns, and a rapidly changing technology had taken their toll on black public education. Severely overcrowded classrooms, the displacement of black teacher role models, and limited educational and job options caused academic and occupational under-achievement—especially in poor communities and large inner city schools. Minimal standards prevailed, while busing and the resultant white backlash sowed more seeds of disharmony.

The Independent School

Public schools, at their best, shine. Experimental academic high schools in many urban areas have proven to be a boon to the fast-learning student while comprehensive high schools in affluent suburbs regularly turn out high scorers on merit scholarship tests.

Every city can boast of one or several model schools. But every city, too, can point to educational disaster areas, which are shunned by elected officials and hated by teachers, students, and parents alike. Unable to supply even basic educational needs, these schools induce mental dead weight by denying students the dignity, discipline, and challenge of scholarship. Because of this academic abandonment, many students are labeled, often unfairly, as "uneducable" or "learning disabled."

Disillusionment with this situation has given way to self-help action in low-income neighborhoods from Boston to Los Angeles. Neighborhood-based independent pre-schools, elementary, middle, and high schools are springing up in areas where public school systems have turned their backs on education. Operating almost exclusively on the monies collected from tuition and modest community fundraising, this private school network has become a viable option for low-income parents concerned about securing quality educations for their children. Having a choice, it has been revealed, has given these families a feeling of dignity and self-worth.

The neighborhood school participation process heightens

the family's feeling of dignity, self-worth, and achievement. Thus, not only do parents raise money to pay for quality schools, they also are relied on to donate paper, pencils, typewriters, and other supplies that are sometimes outside of the school's budget. This sense of involvement and shared desire to elevate the lifestyle of the next generation has motivated many families to pool their resources for the common good of the community.

The Neighborhood Option

In 1983, the National Center for Neighborhood Enterprise (NCNE) conducted a sample survey of more than 200 independent community-based schools nationwide that are developing an alternative education for blacks, Hispanics, American Indians, and Asian children from both urban and rural environments. Many, such as the Owl School in Washington, D.C., feature multi-cultural, accelerated education environments that mingle affluent suburban youngsters with low-income, inner city young people. Although some of these schools are housed in substandard physical plants, the quality of instruction and the responsiveness of the children remain high.

An area of commonality in all of the surveyed schools is the regularly scheduled classroom study of the students' cultural and ethnic backgrounds—a concept rarely practiced in most public schools. These teachings contribute to a wholeness of character that lends itself to fuller student participation and receptivity. The average curricula also emphasize mathematics, computer literacy, and foreign language instruction.

The independent community-based schools are all models of self-reliance. The students, teachers, administrators, and parents involved in these efforts have made a conscious decision to go their own way in pursuit of excellence, no matter what the hardship.

At a special 1983 conference on neighborhood-based independent schools sponsored by NCNE, other data compiled in the neighborhood school sample survey was presented.

Randolph Tobias, associate dean of the faculty at Queens College pointed out that "some [of the schools presented here] are religious-based, some nationalistic, and some are preppy. A common thread is believing we can do something better than the public schools. There are needs that our populations have that we can fill better than the public schools."

A parade of independent administrators and teachers underscored Tobias' remarks by speaking of their success in not only providing a strong basic education but also in forging links between warring factions within a community. Reaching out to troubled youths who have become gang members and alcohol and drug abusers has become an important factor in turning negative community energy into a positive force that reaps benefits for the entire neighborhood. Instances were cited of former gang members volunteering their time to convert old buildings into community schools.

Conference Recommendations

Specific recommendations were made at the NCNE Conference on Neighborhood-Based Independent Schools that would both solidify the strength of, and give higher visibility to, local independent schools around the nation.

They include:

- Statewide federations of independent schools should be encouraged so that a nationwide consortium of community-based schools might eventually be established. The consortium could be the conduit for exchanging information, resource-sharing, and public information regarding independent school activities.
- A national archive of curriculum material and historical docu-

ments should be established so that those who wish to learn about the history of independent schools and how to emulate successful examples can come to study.

- Ideas should be developed for starting enterprises that can be associated with the schools, operated by the parents, and subsequently incorporated into the neighborhood economy.
- An umbrella organization should be formed to take advantage of low group-insurance rates that might be offered as a fringe benefit to school staffs.

The Action Agenda

Neighborhood self-help responses to the public school dilemma, at minimum, have increased the educational opportunities available to low-income minority pupils. More often than not, created by frustrated parents at great personal sacrifice, independent neighborhood schools have made a concerted effort to make education live for students who had forgotten, or had never known, the thrill of scholastic challenge.

The financial hardships incurred by the parents of these children is self-evident. Working multiple jobs, carving up lean welfare checks, and borrowing from family and friends seems an unfair burden to place on already hard-pressed low-income families opting to better themselves through nonpublic education. With statistics available showing that many students enrolled in community-based schools are outperforming their public school counterparts, the groundwork has already been laid for future generations to climb out of poverty and welfare dependency with relevant educations. For this reason alone, a voucher system should be established that would give money directly to impoverished parents who have been denied access to fee-charging private schools. Such a system would be a fair way of getting a return on the taxes spent to support public education.

An argument may also be made that the more educated our youth, the less likely their gravitation to crime and the unemployment rolls—two areas that cost governments dearly in social welfare and maintenance programs.

CASE STUDY #3:

IVY LEAF SCHOOL

Reading, Writing, and Relevance

One of the jewels in the crown of community-based black independent schools is the Ivy Leaf School of Philadelphia, Pennsylvania. Starting as a nursery/pre-kindergarten with 17 pupils in 1965, it has expanded to four locations, added 8 grades and, today, boasts an enrollment of over 700 students.

"We have grown because we provide a high-quality academic experience that allows our students to compete in any environment," explained Liller Green, co-founder of Ivy Leaf.

She along with her husband, William Green, opened Ivy Leaf because of dissatisfaction with many current public school standards, and frustration over long waiting lists encountered at the area's quality private schools.

From the beginning, the goal of the school was to create an environment where a comprehensive education would stimulate and challenge the children.

"We had to create an environment where black children would be taught to be proud of themselves and their heritage. We had to teach them that they *could succeed* before society had the opportunity to teach them that they *could not*. We stress both a strong academic program *and* a strong social program," said Liller Green.

The quality of the educational program, the caring attitude of the administration and staff, and the positive development of the pre-school students convinced parents to send their children to Ivy Leaf. Within three years, Ivy Leaf was filled to capacity with 50 students.

In 1971, the Greens purchased another building to extend their program from pre-school through fourth grade. Ivy Leaf's emphasis on reading and mathematical concepts resulted in 85 percent of its students scoring above the national average on the California Achievement Tests.

The continuing surge of parent support made it necessary for the Greens to open two other facilities to accommodate the swiftly growing student roster. By 1982, Ivy Leaf had expanded to eight grades. Parents, who always played a part in the school's expansion and growth, raised $30,000 to purchase 24 computers that are now being used in Grades 2 through 8. A new science laboratory was constructed in 1983 complete with 10 more new computers.

Students are taught reading according to their reading levels regardless of grade level. Within the classrooms, students are given individual instruction in mathematics. All students must meet specific requirements before passing to the next grade level.

In addition to helping students acquire skills that will help them to think critically, Ivy Leaf also teaches them to appreciate the arts and humanities in the areas of literature, music, dance, and poetry. The teaching of proper nutritional habits and physical education activities are incorporated into the curricula to impress upon the students the importance of a healthy environment. A sense of community and social responsibility is also nurtured through the students' participation in neighborhood projects that benefit the larger community.

With the idea of giving students firsthand knowledge about the business world so that they might be inspired to become entrepreneurs themselves, Ivy Leaf joined with the National Center for Neighborhood Enterprise (NCNE) during the 1984–85 school year to create the Ivy Leaf School Smoke Detector Project.

The main purpose of the business development curriculum was to give the students a practical, "hands-on" entrepreneurial experience in selling smoke detectors and other home safety devices that would touch on every aspect of business formation and operation.

Youngsters were employed during the summer and fall by the project as smoke detector sales staff and installers. With the assistance of area businesspersons, the active support of the Philadelphia Deputy Fire Commissioner, and the participation of the Ivy Leaf school administrators, the smoke detectors project was a successful enterprise that received citywide praise for its efforts.

The young entrepreneurs in Philadelphia sold over 1,700 smoke detectors and grossed more than $16,000 in sales during the first three months of operation. Most of the sales and installations were in low-income neighborhoods.

The Ivy Leaf tradition of devising curricula to stimulate young minds is symbolic of the innovative educational approaches available at independent community-based alternative schools nationwide.

Completely self-supporting, Ivy Leaf has a staff of 80 persons. It charges a $1,600 yearly tuition that is well below the $3,0000-$4,000 range of comparable private schools in the Philadelphia area. Some low-income parents have, with the cooperation of the Greens, been able to work as staff in exchange for a tuition-free education for their children. Significantly, a large percentage of the parents are teachers in the Philadelphia Public School System.

Ivy Leaf's eighth grade graduates are sought after by some of the most prestigious private schools in the nation. Approximately half of the graduates are placed in the top academic schools in Philadelphia. Many receive full scholarships to private institutions such as Andover Phillips Academy in Andover, Massachusetts.

These achievements echo the guiding philosophy of Liller

Green: "Black children can consistently achieve a high standard of academic excellence. Educators need to become bolder in their quest for answers to the crises in education. We need to be willing to change and provide opportunities to meet new challenges."

SIX

Making It All Happen

By Glenn C. Loury

Black Americans now confront a great challenge and an enormous opportunity. The black struggle for equality in American society, born in the dark days of slavery and nurtured with the courage and sacrifice of generations who would not silently accept second-class citizenship, now threatens to falter and come to a stop—short of its historic goal. Throughout America, in the rural counties of the Black Belt, in the slums of Harlem, in North Philadelphia, on the west side of Chicago, on he east side of Detroit, in south-central Los Angeles, in the ghettos of Houston and Oakland and Newark, and in scores of smaller cities and towns, literally millions of blacks live in poverty and, all too often, despair.

The great challenge facing black America today is the task of taking control of its own future by exerting the necessary leadership, making the required sacrifices, and building the needed institutions so that black social and economic development becomes a reality. No matter how windy the debate becomes among white liberals and conservatives as to what should be done, meeting this self-help challenge ultimately depends on black action.

It is unwise (and dangerous) to suppose that any state or federal government would, over the long haul, remain sufficiently committed to such a program of black revitalization. It is to make a mockery of the ideal of freedom to hold that, as free men and women, blacks must nonetheless sit back and wait for white Americans, of whatever political persuasion, to come to their rescue. A people who languish in dependency have surrendered their claim to dignity. A genuinely free people must accept responsibility for their fate. Black America's political leaders have failed to face up to this fact.

One way of framing the choice now confronting blacks is to ask: "What does it mean today to be an advocate for the poor?" The essays collected in this book offer a different answer to this question than that provided by those most widely recognized as "black leaders." The central theme here is that poor black people have the capacity to begin to make fundamental improvements in their lives, given the opportunity. An advocate for the poor, from the perspective of the authors collected here, is one who provides the means for poor people to help themselves develop to their full potential. He is not someone who perpetuates the dependency of poor people, teaching them by his example that their only option is to hold out their hands to accept gifts from others. There are some essential elements of this new approach to the problems of the poor that should be emphasized.

- *It is distinctly less adversarial in political tone, but retains a sense of urgency about solving the problems of poor blacks.* It is now a vital necessity to move beyond the politics of outstretched-hand dependency to a position where black Americans can stand on their own two feet and hold their heads up. This is urgent both for blacks and for America. It is profoundly unhealthy that the core of our largest cities should, as a permanent matter, be occupied by people without hope or a viable stake in the country's economic and political system. The national interest requires that the United States not become a nation of haves and have-nots. Ours cannot be a great nation while human resources are wasted in blighted inner cities from coast-to-coast.

- *Its focus is on "win-win" rather than "win-lose" solutions.* The authors have focused on creating opportunities for the poor that build on indigenous skills—solutions by which poor people can gain without others having to lose. The welfare state is divisive because of its implication that the poor are entitled to their "fair share" at the expense of the economically better off. Economic growth permits everyone to win. Development of the existing skills and capabilities of those living in poverty is better than paying "professionals" public monies that should be channeled toward self-help efforts.

- *Securing dignity for the poor is an important benefit of making a community more responsible for its own destiny.* For example, those who have observed Kimi Gray's work at the Kenilworth-Parkside public housing project in Washington, D.C., have noticed that the people in her development have dignity and a feeling of self-respect. Achieving this goal is doing much more for people than giving them money. It is a sense of empowerment, the feeling that they can exert some influence over what happens to them, that has helped to reduce crime, vandalism, and teenage pregnancies.

- *The authors of this book accept the proposition that new ideas can change people's lives.* Over the last few decades, advocates for the poor have had a one-note preoccupation with demands for more government aid. New ideas are being put forward here that have the potential to bring about basic changes in the way people think about and approach the problem of poverty.

Notice the optimism, energy, and dynamism of the people whose solution-oriented programs and projects have been discussed in earlier chapters. Their focus is on initiating positive self-help courses of action that lead to improvement, and not on the passive recitation of negative statistics of suffering and poverty that have become the stock in trade of most "poverty advocates." Their business is helping people help themselves; not showing people how to ingratiate themselves to a bureaucracy in order to get a handout. Their concern is not to characterize the poor as victims in order to get the pity (and hence dollars) of the rest of America. These positive activists look upon the condition of the poor with an eye for opportunities that exploit the existing strengths of their communities.

The standard racism litany has gotten short shrift in this book. The authors whose ideas are conveyed here are not interested in placing blame on white people, but in identifying and taking up the responsibilities of black people. They recognize that only in this way can the problems of poor black people be solved.

Clearing the Agenda

It is the power of these ideas that will bring about the transformation in poor people's lives that must take place if America is to successfully grapple with this dilemma. It is not sufficient to oppose efforts that have failed in the past. Of course that is necessary, but it is not enough. Neither is "caring" enough. The often encountered practice of declaring oneself morally superior by virtue of having cared more or cared earlier is insufficient. It is almost morally irrelevant in these critical times to declare that one cares. What matters is whether or not one has ideas and is prepared to act on them to improve the circumstances of the poor.

In order for the black self-help movement to flourish and prosper, several impediments must be dealt with. One is legislators who are unwilling to consider efforts that would spur self-help activities, such as setting up enterprise zones in areas of high urban unemployment.

Another major impediment comes from those who graft their interests on to those of the economically disenfranchised. A poor people's march is seldom held without the participation of radical feminists, gay rights activists, environmentalists, and communist apologists who have twisted the misfortune of the inner city poor to their own ends.

Yet another major obstacle to the goal of black empowerment is the quality of leadership supplied by many black elected officials. In local, state, and federal elections around the country, the black masses are constantly told that sending a black elected official to the mayor's office, the state capital, or Congress will lead to the solution of their plight. Yet, in many big cities around the country where blacks are in positions of power, the same lack of economic development can be seen in black ghettos as can be seen in white-controlled cities. It is not suggested that all black politicians are unworthy of their people's support, but there should be mechanisms to discipline indifferent political leaders so that they would be forced to adopt positions and pursue programs that contribute to the economic and social advancement of their constituents. The sad fact is that these disciplining forces are few in number.

Unfortunately, poor blacks seldom seem willing to exercise this kind of critical judgment. Black elected officials who have done little, other than parrot the lines of white liberals, seem to be regularly re-elected to their positions of leadership in spite of poor performance. This kind of behavior by a black politician is a luxury that poor blacks cannot afford. Because of the long history of racism, many blacks decide their vote on the basis of group solidarity, rather than a common-sense evaluation of a politician's on-the-job performance. Many black incumbents seem immune to challenge by other blacks, as it is easy to describe the challenger as somehow being "a white man's nigger."

The rascal incumbent should, of course, be voted out of office. But, even before that, poor blacks should structure an ongoing system of monitoring a politician's day-to-day performance. Regularly scheduled public political forums and community-based newsletters are but two examples of how to match deed with need.

Understanding Community Capabilities

John L. McKnight, associate director of the Center for Urban Affairs and Policy Research at Northwestern University, has made an accurate assessment of how our society views its poor: "What we have done for many poor people is to say to them you are sentenced to being a consumer and a client, you are denied the privileges to create, to solve problems, and to produce; you have the most degraded status our society will provide."[27]

McKnight, recounting an experience he had in a low-income community during the 1960s, tells of "poverty experts" who came into a town of 20,000 residents to conduct "needs surveys." All too predictably, they discovered there were severe problems in the areas of housing, education, jobs, crime, and health.

In his role as community organizer, McKnight took note of the "public policy experts" *from both the public and the private sectors*. They included: public housing officials, land clearance experts, housing development counselors, daily living skills advisers, rodent removal experts, weatherization counselors, teacher's aides, audio-visual specialists, urban curriculum developers, teacher trainers, school security advisers, civil rights consultants, job developers, job counselors, job classifiers, job location specialists, relocation program specialists, job trainees, small business advisers, police aides, correctional system designers, rehabilitation specialists, juvenile counselors, diversion specialists, social workers, psychologists, psychiatrists, health outreach workers, health educators, sex educators, environmental reform workers, caseworkers, home budget management trainers, lead paint inspectors, skills trainers, and administrators and managers to coordinate all of these activities. In short, overkill. McKnight termed this situation an example of an economic development plan for people who *don't* live in the neighborhood.

McKnight concluded his observation with bull's-eye accuracy:

I know from years in the neighborhoods that we can rely on community creativity. You have heard about it today over and over again. It is the most exciting thing that's happening in America. America is being reinvented little by little in the little places, but there is much more wealth that could be freed up, made available, if we understood that we have a big investment in the poor but their income is radically misdirected into the hands of service professionals.

McKnight's example is all too familiar to those who are aware of the profusion of misdirected and misinformed approaches to "solving" the problems of this country's low-income citizens. This miscalculation of black capabilities is not by any means restricted to white America.

Some of the most eminent black thinkers, with close links to the civil rights establishment, no longer voice the same confidence they once did regarding the capabilities of black people. As noted in Chapter One, a great turning point was reached in the history of black Americans when, in 1934, the brilliant black thinker W.E.B. Du Bois was dismissed from the editorship of the NAACP's organ *Crisis* because of his view that the drive for integration at all costs undermined black people's confidence in their own institutions and capacities. Fearing that the fight against segregation (which he often led) had become a crusade to mix with whites for its own sake, Du Bois wrote: "Never in the world should our fight be against association with ourselves because by that very token we give up the whole argument that we are worth associating with."

Just twenty years after these words were written, however, black psychologist Kenneth Clark managed to convince a majority of the Supreme Court Justices that segregation was inherently damaging to the personalities of black children. Unless whites were willing to mix with blacks, Clark seemed to argue, the result would inevitably be that black children would suffer self-image problems. This intellectual perspective, which says that development and self-respect for blacks is inherently impossible without "integration," might itself be considered damaging to the personalities of black children. Of this perspective Floyd McKissick once noted sarcastically that it seems to mean "if you put Negro with Negro you get stupidity." Such apparent expressions of black insecurity and inferiority bore out Du Bois' fears. Seemingly, the civil rights struggle moved from ending *de facto* segregation to forced racial mixing, rejecting the possibility of beneficial association by blacks with blacks.

This lack of confidence voiced by the black intelligentsia is extended to the capacity of black institutions to successfully confront the development problems that black people face. Many examples of this could be given, but one in the area of education should make the point. An earlier chapter tells of the potential offered by the development of independent black schools in the inner cities. These schools are examples of how the education of poor black children can be advanced with very limited resources, when there are parents and teachers willing to make education an urgent priority. Yet so deeply entrenched is the civil rights mentality that in some communities black children are permitted to languish with limited skills while their "advocates" seek ever more far-fetched versions of "integration."

In 1977, black parents in Ann Arbor, Michigan, faced a difficult educational problem. Their children in the early grades were not learning how to read, though white students were. A group of civil rights lawyers and educators convinced these parents to sue the public schools for discriminatory practices because white teachers in Ann Arbor failed to take account of the fact that the black children spoke a distinct dialect of the English language called "black English." Two years later, a federal judge ordered the Ann Arbor schools to provide teachers with sensitivity training in "black English," so as to better teach reading to the black students. Today, after the court order, it appears that young blacks in Ann Arbor continue to lag far behind their white counterparts in reading ability—but they have won their discrimination lawsuit and are duly instructed by teachers "sensitized" to their "foreign" dialect.

All of this would be amusing if it weren't so tragically sad. Civil rights advocates won a symbolic victory, but how did the children profit? While years of legal wrangling went on, the opportunity for the Ann Arbor community to address directly the needs of the poor black students went unexploited. Apparently, it never occurred to the parents or their "advocates" that, rather than cast their problem as one of discrimination, their children might benefit more from a straightforward effort to tutor them in reading and English. With 35,000 students at the University of Michigan's Ann Arbor campus, a sizable number of whom are black, sufficient volunteers for such a tutoring effort could have been found. The fact that such an effort never materialized suggests the kind of intellectual malaise which Du Bois warned of a half-century ago. This example illustrates the importance of exploring ideas and alternative options for the purpose of attaining a worthwhile goal.

Blacks must examine their past objectively, taking what is valuable from it and rejecting those notions that have proven unworkable. Over many decades and under much more adverse circumstances, blacks have struggled to make impressive progress without the benefit of the civil rights laws and welfare transfers that now exist.

There are many examples of the impressive accomplishments attained by preceding generations under difficult conditions. The literacy rate among blacks rose dramatically after emancipation, though free public schools were virtually nonexistent. Independent black businesses and entire towns flourished in the late 19th century. Despite the terrible economic and social oppression to which slaves were subjected, modern research has shown that they created a vibrant family, religious, and cultural tradition that continues to enrich black America to this day.

The kind of social dislocation and family instability that plagues today's black ghettos was virtually unknown among the black migrant communities in the North in the early years of this century. In 1925 Harlem, 85 percent of black families were intact while single teenaged mothers were a rarity. In Buffalo, NY, in 1910, blacks exhibited similar strong family structures, this notwithstanding the virulent racism faced at the time. Without liberal apologists to tell them what little they could do for themselves or how inevitable their misery, poor black folk in years past were able to maintain their communities to establish a firm foundation for their children's progress.

The Challenge

This heritage is the underpinning of a collective black strength waiting to be tapped today. A dynamic and continuing process of economic, political, and social development must be initiated. Preceding chapters have outlined the components of an economic rejuvenation process that could launch such a large-scale self-help movement. To be successful, however, these suggested programs must be built upon, expanded, revised, and adapted to the varying conditions of local communities nationwide. The time is ripe for blacks to spearhead such an effort. With everything to gain and little to lose, a spirit of black adventurism could lift the community beyond dependency to self-sufficiency.

The question, though, is often asked whether blacks have the intellectual predisposition and political savvy needed to bring this about. Much of the current black leadership, in the civil rights organizations as well as in the halls of Congress, remains wedded to an outmoded conception of the black condition. Theirs is too much the story of discrimination, repression, hopelessness, and frustration; and too little the saga of uplift and genuine empowerment, whether others cooperate or not. This narrow intellectual perspective requires blacks to present themselves to American society as permanent victims, incapable of advance without the help of benevolent whites. By evoking past suffering and the current deprivations experienced by the ghetto poor, some black leaders feed this guilt and, worse, the pity of the white power brokers.

The idea that whites are omnipotent and also responsible for the solution of blacks' problems is one of those unworkable, even dangerous, notions that must be banished from the black mind. This shifting of responsibility onto the shoulders of white America runs the risk of persuading the black individual that he or she can do nothing about his or her situation because the history and ongoing consequences of racism will prevent any progress from occurring. This type of thinking also runs the risk of convincing black communities as a whole that, through collective action, the only thing they can achieve is the election of one of their own to public office—a worthy goal, but hardly the stuff of which economic development is made.

Positive, workable ideas are of crucial importance in any effort to change the current state of black America. To paraphrase those advocates of healthful eating, "You are what you *think!*" To hold the view that nothing positive can occur for poor blacks until the government undertakes the responsibility is to demean black people and make of them witless drones, accomplices in their own victimization. This idea is morally unacceptable. Blacks must not allow themselves to become ever ready doomsayers, always alert to exploit black suffering by offering it up to sympathetic whites as a justification for pressing black demands. This view of how to attain black progress—a view which literally capitalizes on misery by playing on pity—is unbecoming of black America's proud heritage.

Along with economic issues, rethinking how to use political power more effectively should also be at the top of the black agenda for progress. New, non-traditional political approaches should be considered on their merits, rather than rejected categorically.

Unfortunately, this is not the case today. Those blacks who are fed up with welfare state handouts and who are sympathetic to ideas of self-help, business creation, and reliance on the private sector are given a hard way to go. They are called "conservative ideologues" by those incumbent black politicians who, for a quarter of a century have done little more than repeat, ever more loudly, their demand that government ride in on a white horse to save their constituents. In doing so, these "leaders" hope to secure their positions against challenge from other blacks with different ideas. If they succeed in this, they will simultaneously succeed in insulating themselves from the forces of accountability, permitting them to pursue whatever agenda may spring to their minds, whether or not such pursuits actually produce results for their people.

It is not hard to see who will be the losers if they succeed.

The stakes are too high for this kind of unaccountable political behavior on the part of black leadership to continue. America is undergoing a fundamental political change—some say an historic realignment between the Democrats and the Republicans. It may be too early for such conclusions, but it does seem clear that the bulk of the electorate—Democrat and Republican—has moved to the right in recent years. While this has happened, black political spokespersons have steadfastly clung to views and policies found only in the far left precincts of the liberal Democrats. Mr. Reagan won a landslide reelection victory of historic proportions even as black leaders were decrying his administration and calling for its "elimination from the face of the earth." It would seem that black leaders have two alternatives: to wait, hoping that the country will move in their direction again, or to develop a program that addresses the problems of the black poor from a broader base of political support.

Of these alternatives, only the second represents responsible leadership at this juncture. And it is this alternative that is explored in specific terms in this book. But the question remains, and it has not been answered in the time since President Reagan's second inauguration: Can black leaders adapt to these changing circumstances? If not, then the black masses should vote them out of office without regret.

The 1984 Reagan landslide should not be interpreted as proving that blacks will always be losers in the political arena. The last election merely proved that there was too little diversity in the politics of the black community. Black America has become too closely attached to the welfare mentality. This position has come under increasing attack in public discussions of policy, and has many fewer adherents today than it did ten or twenty years ago. In this volume, and in the political and business activities of many blacks around the country, another approach, at once more dignified, more politically viable, and in the long run, more promising, is being advanced. Black people owe it to themselves to give this alternative approach a chance.

There is a battle of ideas, a partisan battle, being waged to determine the future course of domestic and foreign policy. Just as the War on Poverty was born out of the ideas about helping the poor in the early 1960s, the steps taken for the remainder of this century towards dealing with poverty will depend on the ideas now being considered in the wake of the failures of earlier poverty programs.

All the participants in this struggle over ideas are not disinterested observers. Some of them earn their livelihoods and garner their prestige from the current way in which our country chooses to approach the problems of the poor. There are those who have a vested interest in welfare state dependency and in the *client* relationship of the poor to the rest of society. There are those whose anti-market sentiments will not permit them to try opportunity society solutions because somebody might make some money in the process. These hidden agendas need to be dealt with openly so that those for whom the struggle against poverty is being waged can make their own judgments concerning what is in their best interests.

The Action Agenda

The problems of the black poor—economic, social, educational, and political—are enormous. They are not going to be solved with the stroke of a pen, not even the president's pen, and they are not going to be solved soon. No one should suppose that this challenge will be easily or simply met.

Black America cannot lift itself by its bootstraps into great wealth overnight. But there is a great unexploited potential for change at the level of the black individual and the local black community. In the current environment, it is evident that blacks must exploit this dormant opportunity. Self-help projects must be initiated as a matter of necessity. Blacks must abandon the pernicious and self-destructive tendency to arbitrarily empower the "man" with ultimate control over their community.

Precisely because racism is a fact of life not likely to disappear soon, *all* blacks are "in the same life boat." This being the case, it is in an individual's interest to contribute time and resources to the advancement of those least well-off in the community. It is politically and morally irresponsible to sit back in disgust, as many civil rights veterans are fond of doing, constantly decrying the problems, doing little or nothing to solve them, shouting epithets and threats at whites who grow weary of being "generous and understanding," while the black poor sink deeper and deeper into despair.

It is crucial that blacks not become so caught up in seeking welfare state handouts that they lose their own souls. The very important, but essentially private, matter of what indignities ancestors suffered because of their race must not be allowed to become a vehicle for cheap brokering with the welfare state. The generations of blacks who suffered under Jim Crow deserve something more than simply having their travails used as an excuse for current failures. Past sufferings should not be hauled out to gain guilt money. Such a posture is pitiful and unbecoming of black America's proud heritage. Dependency, even when one is dependent on sympathetic and generous souls, is destructive of dignity.

It *is* okay to win.

NOTES

1. Yancey, R. J. *Federal Government Policy and Black Business Enterprise* (Cambridge, MA: Ballinger Publishing Co., 1974), p.9.

2. Kluger, R., *Simple Justice* (New York: Alfred A. Knopf, 1976), p. 38.

3. Franklin, V.P., *Black Self-Determination* (Westport, Conn.: Lawrence Hill and Co., 1984), p. 143.

4. DeSane, J., *Analogies and Black History: A Programmed Approach* (Teaneck, NJ: DeSane and Associations, 1983), pp. 30–33.

5. Bennett, L. *Before the Mayflower, A History of Black America* (Chicago, Il: Johnson Publishing Co., 1969), p. 287.

6. See Chapter Three.

7. Warren, D. and Warren, R. "Helping Networks: How People Cope with Problems in the Metropolitan Community, Final Report," Monograph Project 3-ROI-MH-2498, National Institute of Mental Health, December 31, 1976.

8. Embree, E. *American Negroes: A Handbook* (New York: The John Day Co., 1942), p. 43.

9. Bardolph, R., *The Negro Vanguard* (New York: Vintage Books, 1961), p. 275.

10. "The Top 100 Black Businesses," *Black Enterprise*, June 1985, pp. 97–105.

11. Henderson, L. J. "Black Business Development and Public Policy," in J. Williams (Ed.) *The State of Black America 1983* (Washington, D.C.: National Urban League, 1983), pp. 155–185.

12. U.S. Bureau of the Census, "Household and Family Characteristics," *Current Population Reports*, 1971 and 1981.

13. National Urban League Research Department, "Fourth Quarter, 1983," *Quarterly Economic Report*, February, 1984.

14. Young, A.M., "Fewer Students in Work Force as School Age Population Declines," *Monthly Labor Review*, July 1984, pp. 34–37.

15. Woodson, R.L. (Ed.) *Youth Crime and Urban Policy* (Washington, D.C.: American Enterprise Institute, 1981).

16. U.S. Department of Labor, "Employment of High School Graduates and Dropouts, *BLS Special Labor Force Report*, October 1971, No. 145.

17. Young, A. M., "Youth Labor Force Marked Turning Point in 1982," *Monthly Labor Review*, August 1983, pp. 29–32.

18. National Advisory Committee Black Higher Education and Black Colleges and Universities, *Still a Lifeline: The Status of Historical Black Colleges and Universities* (Washington, D.C.: U.S. Department of Education, June 1980).

19. *The Decline in Black Participation in Graduate and Professional Education* (Washington, D.C.: U.S. Department of Education, October 1980).

20. Fleming, J., *Blacks in College* (New York: Josey-Bass, 1985).

21. Hill, R.B., *Informal Adoption Among Black Families* (Washington, D.C.: National Urban League Research Department, 1977).

22. U.S. Bureau of the Census, "Daytime Care of Children: October 1974 and February 1975, *Current Population Reports*, October 1976.

23. Hill, R. B., *Economic Policies and Black Progress* (Washington, D.C.: National Urban League Research Department, 1981).

24. Evaxx, Inc., "A Study of Black American's Attitudes Toward Self-Help." Unpublished report prepared for the American Enterprise Institute, August 1981.

25. Franklin, V.P., *Black Self-Determination* (Westport, Ct: Lawrence Hill and Co., 1984), pp. 168–169.

26. *Ibid.*, p. 168.

27. McKnight, J., speech given at the Revitalizing Our Cities Conference, Fund for an American Renaissance, Washington, D.C. August 1985.

ABOUT THE AUTHORS

Bill Alexander is a freelance writer/editor who has written scores of articles for magazines and newspapers over the past 15 years. He is also a former scriptwriter of *Patches*, an Emmy Award-winning children's show that aired on PBS. He has edited his own magazine and, for several years, worked as a broadcast journalist/producer for such companies as NBC and the Westinghouse Broadcasting Company.

Robert B. Hill is currently adjunct fellow at the National Center for Neighborhood Enterprise. He previously was senior research associate at the Bureau of Social Science Research, Inc., a policy research institute in Washington, D.C. Prior to joining the Bureau, Dr. Hill was director of research for the National Urban League, where he authored the landmark work, *Strengths of Black Families*.

Glenn Loury is professor of Political Economy and Afro-American Studies at Harvard University's John F. Kennedy School of Government. Previously, Dr. Loury taught economics at the University of Michigan and Northwestern University. He has contributed many articles to magazines, scholarly journals, newspapers, and books.

Paul Pryde, Jr. is president of Pryde, Roberts and Company, a consulting firm that plans and designs enterprise development programs for communities wishing to increase private investment employment and economic activity. He has lectured extensively on the potential and limitations of enterprise zones. His articles and publications on development lending include *Development Finance: A Primer for Policy Makers*, a three-volume monograph on the federal role in stimulating improved patterns of economic development.

Robert L. Woodson is the founder and president of the National Center for Neighborhood Enterprise. He is also chairman of the Council for a Black Economic Agenda. Prior to forming his own organization, he was resident fellow at the American Enterprise Institute. Mr. Woodson is the author of *A Summons to Life: Mediating Structures and the Prevention of Youth Crime* and the editor of *Youth Crime and Urban Policy: A View From the Inner City.*